THE CENTURY BIBLE

General Editors

H. H. ROWLEY
M.A., B.LITT., D.D., LL.D., F.B.A. (Old Testament)

MATTHEW BLACK
D.D., D.LITT., F.B.A. (New Testament)

1 and 2 Thessalonians

THE CENTURY BIBLE
NEW SERIES
Based on the Revised Standard Version

---

1 and 2 Thessalonians

Edited by
A. L. MOORE
Wycliffe Hall, Oxford

the Attic Press, Inc.
GREENWOOD, S. C.

THOMAS NELSON AND SONS LTD

36 Park Street London W1
P.O. Box 336 Apapa Lagos
P.O. Box 25012 Nairobi
P.O. Box 21149 Dar es Salaam
P.O. Box 2187 Accra
77 Coffee Street San Fernando Trinidad

THOMAS NELSON (AUSTRALIA) LTD
597 Little Collins Street Melbourne 3000

THOMAS NELSON AND SONS (SOUTH AFRICA) (PROPRIETARY) LTD
51 Commissioner Street Johannesburg

THOMAS NELSON AND SONS (CANADA) LTD
81 Curlew Drive Don Mills Ontario

THOMAS NELSON AND SONS
Copewood and Davis Streets Camden New Jersey 08103

———

© Thomas Nelson and Sons Limited 1969

First published 1969

17 123114 7

PRINTED AND BOUND IN ENGLAND BY
HAZELL WATSON AND VINEY LTD
AYLESBURY, BUCKS

CONTENTS

LISTS OF ABBREVIATIONS

ABBREVIATIONS OF THE BOOKS OF THE BIBLE

OLD TESTAMENT (*OT*)

Gen.	Jg.	1 Chr.	Ps.	Lam.	Ob.	Hag.
Exod.	Ru.	2 Chr.	Prov.	Ezek.	Jon.	Zech.
Lev.	1 Sam.	Ezr.	Ec.	Dan.	Mic.	Mal.
Num.	2 Sam.	Neh.	Ca.	Hos.	Nah.	
Dt.	1 Kg.	Est.	Isa.	Jl	Hab.	
Jos.	2 Kg.	Job	Jer.	Am.	Zeph.	

APOCRYPHA (*Apoc.*)

1 Esd.	Tob.	Ad. Est.	Sir.	S 3 Ch.	Bel	1 Mac.
2 Esd.	Jdt.	Wis.	Bar.	Sus.	Man.	2 Mac.
			Ep. Jer.			

NEW TESTAMENT (*NT*)

Mt.	Ac.	Gal.	1 Th.	Tit.	1 Pet.	3 Jn
Mk	Rom.	Eph.	2 Th.	Phm.	2 Pet.	Jude
Lk.	1 C.	Phil.	1 Tim.	Heb.	1 Jn	Rev.
Jn	2 C.	Col.	2 Tim.	Jas	2 Jn	

ABBREVIATIONS REFERRING TO DEAD SEA SCROLLS

1QIsa	First Isaiah Scroll
1QIsb	Second Isaiah Scroll
1QLevi	Second Testament of Levi
1QpHab	Habakkuk Commentary
1QS	Rule of the Community (Manual of Discipline)
1QSa (= 1Q28a)	Rule of the Community (Appendix)
1Qsb (= 1Q28b)	Collection of Benedictions
1QM	War of the Sons of Light against the Sons of Darkness
1QH	Hymns of Thanksgiving
CD	Fragments of a Zadokite work (Damascus Document)

BIBLIOGRAPHY

COMMENTARIES

C. J. Ellicott, *St. Paul's Epistles to the Thessalonians*, London, 1880 (4th ed.).

J. Denney, *The Epistles to the Thessalonians (Expositor's Bible)*, London, 1892.

G. G. Findlay, *The Epistles to the Thessalonians (C.G.T.)*, Cambridge, 1904.

G. Milligan, *St. Paul's Epistles to the Thessalonians*, London, 1908.

J. Moffatt, in *The Expositor's Greek Testament*, London, 1910.

J. E. Frame, *The Epistles of St. Paul to the Thessalonians (I.C.C.)*, Edinburgh, 1912.

A. Plummer, *A Commentary on St. Paul's First Epistle to the Thessalonians*, London. 1918: *A Commentary on St Paul's Second Epistle to the Thessalonians*, London, 1918.

W. F. Adeney, *Thessalonians and Galatians (Century Bible)*, Edinburgh, undated.

W. Kelly, *The Epistles of Paul the Apostle to the Thessalonians*, London, 1926 (3rd ed.).

E. J. Bicknell, *The First and Second Epistles to the Thessalonians (Westminster Commentary)*, London, 1932.

M. Dibelius, *An die Thessalonicher, I, II. An die Philipper (Handbuch zum Neuen Testament)*, Tübingen, 1937 (2nd ed.).

A. Oepke, *Die kleineren Briefe des Apostels Paulus (Das Neue Testament Deutsch)*, Göttingen, 1949 (2nd ed.).

W. Neil, *The Epistles of Paul to the Thessalonians (Moffatt New Testament Commentary)*, London, 1950.

L. Morris, *The Epistles of Paul to the Thessalonians (Tyndale New Testament Commentaries)*, London, 1956.

B. Rigaux, *Saint Paul, Les Épitres aux Thessaloniciens*, Paris, 1956.

K. Grayston, *Letters of Paul to the Phillippians and Thessalonians*, Cambridge, 1967.

GENERAL

AV	Authorised Version
NEB	New English Bible
RSV	Revised Standard Version
RV	Revised Version
Lake	K. Lake, *The Beginnings of Christianity*, V.
Moffatt, *New Testament*	J. Moffatt, *An Introduction to the Literature of the New Testament* Edinburgh, 1927.
Glasson	T. F. Glasson, *The Second Advent*, London, 1947.
Cullmann	O. Cullmann, *Christ and Time*, London, 1951.
Bultmann	R. Bultmann, *A Theology of the New Testament*, London, 1952.

Taylor	V. Taylor, *Names of Jesus*, London, 1953.
Dibelius, *Paul*	M. Dibelius, *Paul*, London, 1953.
Robinson	J. A. T. Robinson, *Jesus and His Coming*, London, 1957.
Cranfield	C. E. B. Cranfield, *St Mark*, Cambridge, 1959.
Cranfield, *I and II Peter*	C. E. B. Cranfield, *I and II Peter and Jude*, London, 1960.
Ladd	G. E. Ladd, *Jesus and the Kingdom: the Eschatology of Biblical Realism*, New York, 1964.

INTRODUCTION

1. THE BACKGROUND OF THE EPISTLES

THESSALONICA AND THE CHRISTIAN MISSION

Paul, Silas, and Timothy entered Thessalonica early in A.D. 50 more by accident than by their design. Paul had set out on what is called his second missionary journey, apparently intending to revisit the churches already established in western Asia. Ac. 15.36 says that the tour was for this purpose rather than for breaking new ground, and there is no reason to suppose that this does not represent accurately the historical facts. According to the same narrative (Ac. 15.37–40) Paul had chosen Silas as a companion for this tour in preference to Mark, whom Barnabas favoured, and because of this difference of opinion Paul and Barnabas had parted company. During their brief stay in Lystra Paul and Silas encountered Timothy, the son of a Jewish mother and Greek father, 'well spoken of by the brethren at Lystra and Iconium' (Ac. 16.2). He joined the two missionaries and became closely attached to Paul, as we read in later correspondence (e.g. Phil. 2.20–22). It was then that the Holy Spirit began to alter the missionaries' original plans, leading them to undertake no preaching in the provinces of Asia and Bithynia and directing them to new evangelism on the mainland of Greece, specifically in Macedonia (Ac. 16.6–10). Taking ship from Troas and calling *en route* at Samothrace and the port of Neapolis, they soon arrived at Philippi, a city of some importance and a Roman colony since the defeat there of Brutus and Cassius by Antony and Octavian in 42 B.C. Here they experienced difficulties on account of a slave girl from whom Paul had exorcised a 'spirit of divination'. Enraged by their loss, those who had formerly exploited the girl's powers for their own gain dragged the missionaries before the magistrates, laid false but effective charges against them and had them imprisoned and beaten. Following their release the next day Paul and his companions hurried on along the famous Via Egnatia, passing through Amphipolis and Apollonia and arrived in Thessalonica.

Thessalonica (now Salonica) was situated at the head of the Thermaic gulf on the main thoroughfare between Byzantium in the East and Rome in the West. It was of the greatest importance for trade by land and sea and inevitably grew to become the largest and most important city in Macedonia. Cassander is responsible for its name, having called it after his wife. But it is not certain whether the original town of Thermae was expanded and renamed by him or whether he built near the older Thermae a new town which in due course swallowed up the adjacent one. At any rate, Cassander helped to establish the city as an influential and important place. Under the Romans the province of Macedonia was divided into four districts and Thessalonica was the obvious capital of one of these; but its strategic and economic importance elevated it into the seat of the provincial governor and the practical capital of the entire province. In the internal strife which followed Julius Caesar's assassination, Thessalonica had offered its loyalty to Antony and Octavian, the ultimate victors, and the prestige afforded it in return accounts for the degree of self-rule it enjoyed. Some of its coins commemorate its being made a free city, a privilege which allowed it to have its own magistrates (rightly called by Luke in Ac. 17.6 'politarchs'). The city had for long attracted large numbers of Jews into its population (and even into the present century about a quarter of its inhabitants were Jews).

According to the narrative of Ac. 17 what happened after their arrival in this capital city was that the missionaries followed Paul's usual practice of preaching first in the Jewish synagogue. This practice was not only an obviously sensible and fruitful point of departure for preaching the Christian gospel but also conformed with Paul's conviction that the plan of salvation should be unfolded 'to the Jew first and also to the Greek' (Rom. 2.9–10). On three apparently successive sabbath days Paul preached to the congregation 'explaining and proving that it was necessary for the Christ to suffer and to rise from the dead . . .' (Ac. 17.3). The chief success of these evangelistic efforts was a number of converts from the Greek proselyte section of the synagogue (Ac. 17.4 speaks of 'some' Jews, 'a great many' devout Greeks and 'not a few of the leading women'). It is perhaps not surprising that these proselytes proved more amenable than the Jews to the gospel. The fact that they were intentional rather than conventional adherents to Judaism indicates that they were enquiring and thinking people, and Morris (p. 12) is no doubt right in suggesting that 'they were dissatisfied with the low standards of pagan morality and with the idol worship which fostered them. They were attracted by the monotheism and lofty morality of Judaism, but, at the same time, were repelled by its narrow nationalism and ritual requirements. In Christianity they found a faith that satisfied.' The success of this preaching meant a loss of membership to the synagogue, which aroused the bitter jealousy of the Jews, and the missionaries found themselves, as at Philippi, very quickly in trouble. Ac. 17.5–9 record the subsequent events.

The jealous Jews resorted to violence. Conscripting the help of some ruffians they created an uproar throughout the city and set about attacking Jason's house in the hope of finding the missionaries with their host. In fact the missionaries were out, but undeterred by this the Jews dragged Jason himself and a few other unnamed Christians before the civic authorities charging them on two counts: (1) that Jason had harboured those who 'have turned the world upside down', and (2) that they were 'all acting against the decrees of Caesar, saying that there is another king, Jesus' (Ac. 17.6f.), a charge reminiscent of that laid against Jesus himself (Lk. 23.2f.). Probably the Jews did not impress the politarchs as deeply as they had the crowd, for it was considered enough by the authorities that they should 'take security' from Jason and then release them. Many commentators conjecture that the security taken consisted in an undertaking by Jason no longer to harbour these 'seditious' characters, but it is equally possible that they were simply bound over to keep the peace. The latter conjecture would satisfactorily account for the decision to send Paul and Silas away immediately and quietly, and also explain how Paul could confidently look forward, once the excitement had died down, to a return visit (1 Th. 2.17).

Paul and Silas continued along the coast road to Beroea. Here, according to Ac. 17.11, the Jews were 'more noble than those in Thessalonica' and the missionaries had some success amongst them. However, once news of this reached Thessalonica, the Jews there hastened to Beroea and stirred up similar civic uproar as they had already created and found effective in their home town, with the result that Paul immediately set out for Athens and Silas and Timothy followed some time afterwards. Ac. 18.5 suggests that Silas and Timothy met up with Paul after his arrival in Corinth, but from 1 Th. 3.2 it seems reasonable to suppose that Timothy at least joined Paul whilst he was still in Athens, that he was sent back by Paul to discover how things fared in Thessalonica, and that Silas and Timothy—having met up with each other somewhere on the way—arrived together to join Paul after the latter had already begun work in Corinth. (It is not impossible, though it is pure conjecture, that both Timothy and Silas met Paul in Athens (cf. the peremptory summons in Ac. 17.15), and that Timothy was sent off to Thessalonica and Silas was dispatched to Philippi or Beroea for a similar purpose and that they met by prearranged plan when their errands were completed to travel back to Corinth together.)

THE CHARACTER OF THE THESSALONIAN CHURCH
The church was founded in Thessalonica during a very brief and a very troubled stay. Even if Jason's arrest did not follow directly the three weeks' preaching mentioned in Ac. 17.2 (though it is most natural to suppose that it was not long after) it is clear that the missionaries stayed only a few weeks or months (some suggest as long as six months, but the evidence for this is lacking), and that their visit ended in something like pandemonium. By the time he arrived in Corinth, Paul had behind him a series of disturbances and apparent failures at Philippi, Thessalonica, Beroea, and Athens. Small wonder that Paul, being frustrated in his desire to return personally to Thessalonica, at last sent off Timothy to learn of his converts' state and to strengthen their faith. Small wonder either that on Timothy's return with a glowing report of their constant faith and love (1 Th. 3.6) Paul could write from Corinth, 'for this reason, brethren, in all our distress and affliction we have been comforted about you through your faith; for now we live, if you stand fast in the Lord' (1 Th. 3.7f.). Despite the apparent series of failures, Paul had good reason to feel reassured and comforted.

Though the missionaries' stay was short, Paul claims that they preached at Thessalonica with much boldness and despite opposition

(1 Th. 1.5; 2.2), and that converts were made. A few were Jews, most were Gentiles. Ac. 17.4 speaks of the converts from the devout Greeks as 'a great many', but we should probably understand this relatively: the total number of converts is likely to have been fairly small. That they were also fairly poor is indicated by the fact that Paul reckoned the cost of supporting the missionaries would have been to them a substantial burden, which he was at pains to spare them (1 Th. 2.9).

The obvious joy which the news of the Thessalonians' faith and love brought Paul did not detract him from his pastoral task of caring constantly for his flock, and he realized that his converts still had much to learn and were continuously in need of advice and encouragement. After the missionaries' departure there had arisen some sort of persecution of the Christian community (1 Th. 2.14f.), and Paul's letters were written partly to strengthen his converts in their tribulations. Furthermore, in Paul's absence the Jews appear to have started a smear campaign against the apostle, seeking to spread the idea that Paul had had unworthy motives and that his methods and aims were dishonourable. The apostle wrote to deny categorically any such suggestion and to reassure his flock that his entire ministry was blameless, that he proclaimed the truth of God, that his behaviour had been beyond reproach and that he had sought nothing in the way of personal gain or reward. It was clear to the apostle also that his converts still had certain things to learn or to re-learn, and the correspondence arose in part in order to continue the teaching programme which his sudden departure had interrupted.

Amongst the matters which Paul regarded as needing further or repeated teaching were: (1) Christian morality (1 Th. 4.4ff.) and its qualitative difference over against pagan behaviour; (2) the need to be self-supporting and not to depend on others whilst idling one's time and minding other people's affairs (1 Th. 4.9ff.; 2 Th. 3.6ff.); (3) a specific problem concerning the position of Christian dead at the Parousia (1 Th. 4.13ff.); (4) the nature of the present as an eschatological time and the hope in the still future Parousia of Jesus Christ (2 Th. 2); (5) various other minor matters of doctrine, discipline, and behaviour.

It is frequently argued that the early Christian church confidently expected that the Parousia would certainly come within the lifetime of most of its members and that the Thessalonian church, encouraged by Paul, held firmly to this expectation. But as exegesis of the letters will suggest, Paul speaks of many other matters besides the Parousia, does not teach that the Parousia would *certainly* occur in the lifetime of the contemporary generation (though he seems to have thought of this as certainly *possible*), nor does there appear to be anything in the nature of a crisis in the Thessalonian church on account of the failure of the Parousia to happen nor on account of the death of some of their number prior to its coming. What the apostle writes in his letters is precisely what one would expect a responsible pastor to write to new converts who are clearly keen but inexperienced and partly uninstructed. Both letters were written not to deal with some shattering crisis but to praise and rebuke, encourage and advise a church still groping towards full faith and still grappling with the implications of that faith for its life in a pagan and hostile world.

2. THE COMPOSITION OF THE EPISTLES

DATE AND PLACE OF ORIGIN OF I THESSALONIANS

It is generally agreed that the first epistle was written from Corinth in the spring of A.D. 50. If this is true, then it is the earliest of the New Testament writings with the exception possibly of the epistle to the Galatians (according to one view of its date and destination).

The evidence for Corinth as the place of origin is the statement in Ac. 18.5 that Silas and Timothy rejoined Paul in Corinth, and the statement in 1 Th. 3.1f. that Paul was at Athens when he sent off Timothy to inspect and help the Thessalonian church (for since it appears that Paul remained at Athens only a brief time and that the journey to and from Thessalonica would have been by sea at least four days and by land considerably longer, it would seem certain that Paul had moved on to Corinth before Timothy returned with the report which gave rise to this epistle). The arrival referred to in Ac. 18.5 where Timothy, now in company with Silas whom he had supposedly met with on the way, 'arrived from Macedonia' is most probably the occasion when Paul received Timothy's report and decided to write.

Regarding the evidence for the date of A.D. 50, let it be noted that here we enter in part the sphere of conjecture and impression. From Ac. 18.12ff. we learn that 'when Gallio was proconsul of Achaia, the Jews made a united attack upon Paul and brought him before the tribunal . . .'. At some point, therefore, Paul's stay in Corinth coincided with Gallio's proconsulship. From Ac. 18.11 we know that Paul remained in Corinth for a year and a half, and from an inscription in Delphi (concerning the answer to a matter referred by Gallio to the Emperor) dated in the twelfth year of the Emperor's tribunicial power (from January A.D. 52 to January A.D. 53) and after Claudius' twenty-sixth acclamation as Emperor (the twenty-seventh was sometime prior to August 52), we gather that Gallio was proconsul certainly in the first half of A.D. 52. (For a discussion of this inscription see K. Lake, *The Earlier Epistles of St. Paul*, pp. 460ff.) The probability seems to be that Gallio became proconsul early in 51 and was nearing the end of his office when he wrote to the Emperor in the early summer of 52 (proconsuls generally took up their appointments in the early summer and held office for one year). We do not know at what point in Paul's stay or of Gallio's proconsulship their paths crossed, but it seems probable from the narrative of Ac. 18 that it was nearing the end of Paul's stay (Ac. 18. 11f. certainly gives this impression) and that it was towards the beginning of Gallio's term of office: but it is not possible to be sure on either point. Quite possibly some sixteen months or so prior to the events recorded in Ac. 18.12ff., namely about April A.D. 50, is the time when Paul wrote his first letter to the Thessalonians.

AUTHORSHIP OF I THESSALONIANS

The genuineness of this letter was practically never in doubt until midway through the last century and then only amongst some of the so-called Tübingen school. It was unchallenged as an epistle of Paul even by Marcion, it is contained in the list of accepted books noted in the Muratorian Fragment and it is mentioned by Irenaeus. It is true that there are few, if any, certain quotations or allusions in the Fathers prior to Irenaeus, but there are passages in Hermas and Ignatius which are reminiscent of sections of 1 Thessalonians, and it is not possible to say that they did not know of its existence.

The internal evidence is even more convincing. The vocabulary certainly appears to be Paul's, for though it is true that some words occur in either or both of these epistles which do not occur elsewhere in the New Testament, or do occur in the New Testament elsewhere but not in Paul's other letters, Frame rightly remarks that this 'indicates not that the language is not Pauline, but that Paul's vocabulary is not exhausted in any or all of the ten letters here assumed as genuine' (*Epistles*, p. 28). Similarly the thoughts expressed and the manner in which they are expressed afford ample evidence that the mind and hand behind the letter are Paul's. In addition, it is fair to say that in view of the contents of the letter, non-Pauline authorship raises more problems and questions than it answers. If it does not stem from the concerned and affectionate pastor and founder of the congregation in Thessalonica, careful of his beloved converts, then it is difficult indeed to see why the epistle says what it does say and why its character is such as it is. A forger would, surely, have had other things to write.

Nevertheless, from the time of Schrader and, more especially, Bauer, it has been held by some that the epistle is spurious and various reasons have been given for this view.

It is suggested that the vagueness of the epistle's teaching accords better with a forger writing 'in a void' than with Paul writing on a particular occasion and addressing a specific situation. However, the receipt of news such as Timothy apparently brought back would be just the occasion for Paul to write and for him to write just the sort of things he does in this letter.

It is argued that the epistle indicates an advancement in Christian faith and life amongst the converts of Thessalonica such as could not be expected after the brief visit of Paul and his companions and the lapse of only a few months or even weeks until the occasion envisaged if Paul wrote from Corinth in A.D. 50. Two answers must be given to that argument. First, the visit might have lasted somewhat longer than the 'three weeks' of Ac. 17.2, but even if, as seems probable, it was only a matter of a few weeks or months,

Paul's industry (cf. 1 Th. 2.9) would see to it that a very great deal would be accomplished in that short while. The results of a few weeks of his night and day toil are not to be compared with those of as many months in many modern, easy-going parochial ministries. Secondly, progress in Christian discipleship cannot be measured only in terms of length of apprenticeship but also and more in terms of the intention and seriousness of the converts. Frame is right to remark that 'the fact that the fame of the little group has spread far and wide . . . is proof not of the long existence of the community but of the intensity and enthusiasm of their faith' (op. cit., p. 38).

Apparent discrepancies between The Acts and 1 Thessalonians have been adduced as evidence of non-Pauline authorship. Ac. 17.2 speaks of three sabbaths, but Paul's references to 'labour and toil', 'night and day' (1 Th. 2.9) suggest, it is said, a longer stay, as also does Phil. 4.16 if this means, as some hold, that the Philippians sent twice to help the apostle at Thessalonica. On the other hand, it is right to note that Phil. 4.16 may well refer to help sent on two occasions but that these were not necessarily both whilst Paul was at Thessalonica. Furthermore, the 'three sabbaths' could indicate an initial ministry to the Jews which was possibly followed by a further Gentile mission, and even if the expression means that the apostle remained but three weeks in Thessalonica this is still time enough for him to speak of labour and toil, if indeed he spent his time ministering the gospel *and* earning his keep. Again Ac. 17.4 says that among the converts were Jews and Gentiles, whilst 1 Th. 1.9 ('turned to God from idols') and 2.14 ('suffered the same things from your own countrymen as they did from the Jews') indicate, it is said, an entirely Gentile community. The letters, however, only indicate (as Ac. 17.4 confirms) that the majority of converts were from a Gentile background and does not at all exclude the presence of some Jewish Christians (and see further on 1 Th. 2.14). It may be noted that whilst there are those who regard divergence from The Acts as an indication of the spuriousness of the epistles to the Thessalonians, there are as many who think such divergencies support its genuineness. Moffatt rightly writes, 'It is capricious to pronounce the epistle a colourless imitation, if it agrees with Acts, and unauthentic if it disagrees' (*New Testament*, p. 71, quoted by Morris, p. 16, n.3).

Some have argued that 2 Th. 2.2 refers to a forged letter purporting to come from Paul and that this must be 1 Thessalonians, which the second letter seeks to correct. This argument need hardly be taken seriously. 2 Th. 2.2 may not refer to an actual forgery but possibly to a false interpretation of a genuine letter (see the commentary *ad loc.*) and what Paul has to say in the second letter by no means contradicts what is said in the first, nor does anything in the first letter, properly understood, amount to the false idea apparently being canvassed by some that 'the day of the Lord has come' (2 Th. 2.2), although an inadequate understanding of the first letter might lead to this.

Bauer maintained that 1 Th. 2.16 is a reference to the fall of Jerusalem and that the letter is therefore post Pauline, post A.D. 70. But again the argument need not be taken too seriously: the reader is referred to the commentary *ad loc.* for the suggested interpretation of the expression 'God's wrath has come upon them at last', which is, at best, slender evidence for such a theory.

In the light of the inadequacy of these objections to genuineness there would seem to be every reason for accepting the weight of tradition and the evidence of internal structure and content and for regarding the letter as authentic to Paul.

DATE AND PLACE OF ORIGIN OF 2 THESSALONIANS

Postponing for a moment the question of authenticity and assuming the letter to be Pauline, it is not unreasonable to suppose that 2 Thessalonians was written from Corinth quite shortly after the first. We learn from Ac. 20.1ff. of a visit to the Macedonian churches by Paul, so the letter is presumably earlier than that. It seems reasonable to suppose that Paul's first letter had not entirely achieved all that he had hoped—though it seems certainly to have counteracted the possible effects of the Jewish propaganda against Paul—and that from reports (arriving by travellers from and through Thessalonica) Paul learned that more could and should be written.

AUTHORSHIP OF 2 THESSALONIANS

As the exegesis offered in the commentary indicates, it is entirely feasible to imagine this second letter addressed to the same community and to a similar situation as that addressed in the first. Its style, language, and character are akin to those of the first, and ancient tradition is similarly firm in accepting the epistle as Pauline. Indeed, in the case of this epistle we find probable quotations in Polycarp (*Ad Phil.* 11.3f.) and possible allusions in Justin (*Dial.* 32.12, etc.) and Ignatius (*Rom.* 10.3). It is included in Marcion's canon and the Muratorian Fragment and, like the first epistle, has been universally accepted from the time of Irenaeus.

Nevertheless, as in the case of the first letter, doubts have in more recent times been cast upon its genuineness. The main reasons for these doubts are:

The eschatological teaching of the second letter is said to be inconsistent with that of the first in certain ways. It is held that in 2 Th. 2.3ff. Paul appeals to teaching formerly given to the converts concerning preparatory signs of the Parousia, whereas in the first letter (1 Th. 5.1–11) Paul taught that the Lord would return suddenly and unexpectedly: there is here, it is argued, an irreconcilable difference. In the first place, however, the ideas of a sudden advent and of preceding signs are certainly not mutually exclusive and their combination is something of a feature of apocalyptic (as, for example, in Mk 13 where we may compare verses 28–31 with verses 32–37). As Paul the pastor knew, it is necessary at one moment to emphasize the one aspect and at another moment to emphasize the other. In the second place, the implication of 1 Th. 5.1, 4 is that the converts knew full well that there are 'signs of the times' and that they must watch and be attentive, that it is precisely because they were aware of the significance of the present time that they would not be overcome by the End as one is caught off guard by a thief.

It is also said by some that the reference to 'Antichrist' in this letter is a sign of spuriousness. Such a reference is said to be without parallel in the New Testament—although this fact alone can have no bearing at all on whether the idea is Pauline or not!—and it is thought by some to imply the particular interpretation of Antichrist in terms of Nero redivivus, which grew up some years after that Emperor's death, and it is therefore far too late to be Pauline. (This application of the Nero redivivus Antichrist legend to 2 Th. 2 goes back to an article by Kern in 1839 and has been accepted by numerous scholars since.) It has, however, been established that the Antichrist legend is far older than the Nero redivivus version and, as the exegesis of chapter 2 in the commentary will seek to indicate, it is very unlikely that the writer of the epistle had in mind any one particular political figure. (In the Introduction to his commentary Rigaux gives an exhaustive treatment of the Antichrist legend and its occurrence in this epistle.) Paul writes of this matter in the second epistle evidently because it had become a real issue due, apparently, to a misunderstanding (wilful or accidental) of Paul's teaching: it had become necessary to explain this aspect of the Parousia more fully.

The literary resemblances (and differences) between the two epistles, it is argued, are hard to account for if the second letter stems from Paul and are more readily explained if the letter was a forgery using the first epistle as its point of departure and basis. Leaving aside the suggestion (proposed by Zahn and regarded as a real possibility by Frame and Neil) that Paul scanned through a copy of the first letter before writing the second, there are two weighty objections to this hypothesis. In the first place, the similarities must not be exaggerated. Some two-thirds of the second letter are new material and the resemblances occur mainly in the general epistolatory outline and in a number of phrases, mostly very short. In the case of certain resemblances it may be that Paul has intended to hark back to his first letter and in other cases, though writing of a matter mentioned in the first letter, actually makes a somewhat different point (as, for example, the reference to his manual labour and self-support which in 1 Th. 2.9 illustrates Paul's concern not to burden his converts but in 2 Th. 3.7ff. is an example of ethical uprightness which the idle members of the congregation should imitate). In the second place, the hypothesis of forgery does not really resolve more questions than it poses—'it is difficult, if not impossible, to determine what the purpose of the forger is and why he hits on 1 as the point of departure for his pseudepigraphon' (Frame, op. cit. p. 51). The suggestion that the 'forgery' was intended to replace the first letter by 'correcting' it is only plausible if it can be proved that the second letter contradicts the teaching of the first, and we have already suggested that such proof is lacking.

It has sometimes been argued that the difference of general tone between the two epistles marks the author of the second as different from that of the first. This need not be taken very seriously. The same writer cannot be required to write always with the same intensity or quality of feeling, cannot always guarantee to be in the same mood nor to be in an exactly similar situation, so that one should actually expect the two letters, if genuine, to display some variation in tone. At the same time, leaving aside the initial section of the first epistle (the personal defence in chapters 1–3) which has no parallel in the second letter, the differences in mood are not very great: there is in both a real affection for the converts and a similar concern for the progress of their faith, hope, and love. If the second deals with offenders somewhat more strictly than the first letter did, may one not say that this is because they were proving more stubborn than was anticipated when the first epistle was written?

Some scholars have suggested that the writer of one or both of the epistles was Silas or Timothy, but positive evidence for this is quite lacking.

THE RELATION OF I THESSALONIANS TO 2 THESSALONIANS
(1) Some scholars argue that 2 Thessalonians is the earlier of the two letters. Their reasons for this view are as follows.

Afflictions being endured by the converts at the time the second letter was written (2 Th. 1.4) are said to be in the past at the time of the first letter (1 Th. 1.6, 2.14f.). Against this, however, it can justly be said that the first letter has very much in mind the thought of continuing affliction to be endured by the Thessalonians (cf. 3.3), and that the purpose of Timothy's mission and of the first letter itself was, in part, to encourage the Christians amidst present and approaching trials.

The introductory formula used in 1 Th. 4.9, 13 and 5.1 ('but concerning') introduces, it is suggested, an answer to some query raised by the Thessalonians in response to a previous letter to them from Paul, namely 2 Thessalonians. But against this argument it may fairly be said that the queries being answered could easily have been brought back to Timothy and, far from being raised by a letter from Paul, could have arisen in the day-to-day life of new converts in a hostile community.

Another argument is that 1 Th. 5.1 is understandable on the basis of 2 Th. 2 but not vice versa. Paul's confidence in the converts' knowledge (1 Th. 5.1), however, could well have been founded on the realization that he had already *spoken* to them on these matters rather than that he had already written about them. 2 Th. 2 is readily understandable as a corrective of false views or false interpretations of what Paul had said or written, and by no means needs to precede 1 Th. 5.1 for either passage to make sense. On the other hand 1 Th. 2.17–3.6 is decidedly *not* understandable if the order of the epistles is reversed.

It is further said that 1 Th. 4.11 speaks of a previous command which in fact we find in 2 Th. 3.10. But 'as we said' in 1 Th. 4.11 most probably refers to the time of Paul's ministry at Thessalonica, and 2 Th. 3.10 in any case refers back to that time and to an oral command ('even when we were with you . . . '). Furthermore 2 Th. 2.15 does seem to point back to the first letter.

The emphasis in 2 Th. 3.17 on Paul's autograph which authenticates the letter is, it is argued, more appropriate in a first letter than in a second. The absence of such an autograph in many letters shows, on the other hand, that it was not an essential feature of a first letter, and its occurrence in 1 C. 16.21 (since this was not the first letter Paul wrote to that church) indicates that it was not inappropriate in a second. Furthermore, the possibility hinted at in 2 Th. 2.2 shows that on this occasion there was a special need to establish genuineness.

It has also been maintained that the 'Jewish' tone of 2 Thessalonians in contrast to the more 'Gentile' tone of the first letter is only understandable if the second was written first when, it is said, the church at Thessalonica was more predominantly Jewish. The evidence, however, for this reconstruction of the initial and later character of the church is wanting and the difference in tone between the two letters should not be exaggerated (see below).

Altogether the argument for reversing the traditional order is weak whereas the reasons for accepting the present order are considerable. (2) Noticing that to some extent the second epistle is more Jewish in character than the first, Harnack, at the beginning of this century, propounded the view that there were in fact two churches in Thessalonica, one predominantly Jewish and the other mainly Gentile. (This view tackles the other end of the problem of the authenticity of the second letter: if one believes it psychologically impossible, as Harnack did, for the two letters to have been written by the same person to the same community, one arrives either at the conclusion that one of the letters is a forgery—which Harnack was convinced was not the case—or at the conclusion that they were not meant for the same people. Neither conclusion, of course, is necessary if one tackles the presupposition concerning psychological impossibility.)

In reply to this theory, two points must be made. First, the differences in emphasis and tone are not very great, nor are they consistently 'Jewish' and 'Gentile'. Secondly, and more significantly, the supposition that Paul reckoned with, accepted and even approved of a church so segregated is almost unthinkable. Harnack understood the charge in 1 Th. 5.27 that the first letter (really to the Gentiles) should be read 'to all' as indicating that there was a Jewish annexe to whom the letter, in courtesy, should also be read. But Paul is more naturally understood here to be referring to recalcitrant members of the one church. Harnack also thought that the variant reading of 2 Th. 2.13 ('a firstfruit' for 'from the beginning') which he accepted, supported his thesis, for whilst the converts in Thessalonica were not the first Pauline converts nor the first Macedonian Christians, it could be said that Jewish converts were the earliest members of the church in Thessalonica. There is, however, little to be said for accepting the variant (see the commentary *ad loc.*) and little to be said for accepting the thesis as a whole. A divided church was, as we learn from 1 C. 1.10ff., the object of Paul's serious admonition, and it seems unthinkable that Paul could have written praises such as are found in both letters (e.g. 1 Th. 1.3, 6ff.; 4.9f.; 2 Th. 1.3f.; 3.4) to a segregated church such as Harnack proposed.

3. THE TEACHING OF THE EPISTLES

The commentary itself will seek to explain what Paul has to say in these two letters, so it would be superfluous even to attempt to summarize his teaching at this point. At the same time it may serve a useful purpose to indicate very briefly what the main themes are which occupy his attention in these epistles.

CHRISTIAN MINISTRY

The work of ministry centres upon the proclamation of the gospel in the power of the Holy Spirit who authenticates the message to the hearer (1 Th. 1.5ff.). Responsible preaching is not mere oratory and certainly not charlatanism (1 Th. 2.3ff.) but is the straightforward narration of that which God has declared and effected in Jesus (1 Th. 2.2). Because of the nature of the message he has to proclaim and because of the nature of the world in which he proclaims it, the minister is involved in afflictions and hardships which also attend those who accept his message (1 Th. 1.6; 2.2; 3.7; etc.). Inasmuch as the minister has an honest and arduous task he can expect to be rewarded by the converts with his keep (1 Th. 2.6), but he might well waive this right out of consideration for the burden this would place on poor disciples, preferring instead to be self-supporting (1 Th. 2.9ff.) and at the same time setting a good example to his converts of industry and endurance (2 Th. 3.7f.). The minister is not 'over' his converts but is much more at their disposal, gentle with them (1 Th. 2.7ff.) and affectionate towards them, deeply concerned with their progress in the Christian faith and life (1 Th. 2.8, 17ff.; 3.1ff.) and constantly remembering them in his prayers (1 Th. 1.2; 3.11; 2 Th. 2.16; 3.5; etc.) as he hopes to be remembered by them in theirs (1 Th. 5.25; 2 Th. 3.3). The ministry in a particular place does not cease when the missionary moves on (by design or by necessity) but the responsible pastor follows up his work with careful teaching and oversight in whatever way is possible to him (1 Th. 2.17–3.5; etc.).

CHRISTIAN FAITH

The objective side of faith is 'our gospel' (1 Th. 1.5) which is at the same time 'the gospel of God' (1 Th. 2.2) and 'the gospel of our Lord Jesus' (2 Th. 1.8), the news that in the advent of Jesus Christ and the events of his life, death, and resurrection the eschatological 'End event' has, in an anticipatory manner, already happened (1 Th. 1.10; 2.12; etc.). On account of this, the possibility of salvation has been realized (1 Th. 2.12; 5.9). The anticipatory occurrence of the 'End' has introduced into the present time an extraordinary tension between what has already happened in a mysterious, hidden, and vicarious way in Jesus Christ (1 Th. 4.14a; 5.10), and what has still to happen in an open, unambiguous, and universal way involving every creature (1 Th. 1.10; 4.14ff.; 2 Th. 1.6ff.). This intolerable tension is in fact endured because it allows the possibility of preaching and the response of faith (cf. 2 Th. 2.6f. and the interpretation of 'what is restraining' suggested in the commentary). The subjective side of faith is acceptance of the gospel proclamation authenticated by real endeavour to 'lead a life worthy of God' (1 Th. 2.12). In short, it is turning to God from idols (1 Th. 1.9): it is the recognition that the proclamation is 'not the word of men . . . but the word of God' (1 Th. 2.13). Faith is not static acquiescence but dynamic acceptance, and therefore Paul can say 'your faith is growing abundantly' (2 Th. 1.3) as he can also speak of 'what is lacking in your faith' (1 Th. 3.10). Faith inevitably gives rise, if it is genuine, to love as its outworking and to hope as its objective (hence the three ideas are brought inextricably together in 1 Th. 1.3 and 2 Th. 1.3f.). Indeed, to be authentic, faith requires ethical obedience as its visible counterpart, and this is something which ultimately God must accomplish in the believer and is therefore to be prayed for (1 Th. 4.1ff.; 5.23; 2 Th. 2.13, 16; 3.3). Why only certain people respond in this positive way to the gospel proclamation is a mystery about which one can only speak in terms of the calling of God (1 Th. 1.4; 2.12; 5.9; 2 Th. 1.11; 2.13). Even in the case of those who reject the message it is not sufficient to speak of their indifference but also of the positive action of God (2 Th. 2.10ff.).

CHRISTIAN HOPE

Paul has much to say in these two letters concerning the future. In 1 Th. 1.10 he describes the Christian's stance as waiting for God's

Son from heaven, and in 2.19, 3.13 and 5.23 speaks of Jesus' future 'coming', indicating that then the ambiguity and equivocation surrounding the proclamation and acceptance of the gospel will be done away and Christians will stand revealed with their Lord (cf. 2 Th. 1.10). Participation in the glory of Christ and appropriation of the verdict of acquittal to be pronounced at the End are anticipated by faith in Christ in the present (1 Th. 1.10; 5.10) but are also only unambiguously and openly revealed at the Parousia of Jesus (2 Th. 1.7, 10). There are many scholars who understand 1 Th. 4.13ff. as meaning that Paul held and taught that the Parousia would definitely occur within his own lifetime and the lifetime of the Thessalonian converts, but it is suggested in the commentary that Paul's hope was not so delimited, that whilst hoping and believing that the Parousia could come very shortly he did not exclude the possibility that it might delay. In one sense the End had already come (hence the relatively easy possibility of misunderstanding Paul, cf. 2 Th. 2.2), but in a hidden form: the revelation in the glory of Jesus of that which had already happened in principle in his humiliation strains to take place (and so must always be regarded as near), and is held back only by the gracious decision of God to allow time for preaching and for faith (2 Th. 2.6ff.). When this revelation is to occur is not known, therefore the Christian must ever be on the alert (1 Th. 5.3ff.). When it does occur the Christians who have already died will be at no disadvantage over against those remaining alive (1 Th. 4.13ff.), and it will be as much a day for the open destruction of the enemies of Christ (behind whom lies a demonic force, 'Antichrist', 2 Th. 2.3ff.) as a day in which the faithful will be rewarded with fellowship with their glorified Lord (1 Th. 4.17; 2 Th. 1.10). The Christian cannot hope necessarily to escape death, but he can and does hope for this union with Christ (1 Th. 5.10), and this hope is his encouragement.

CHRISTIAN LOVE

The Christian life is characterized by love. Paul's own affection for his converts (1 Th. 2.6ff.) was in this respect an example to his flock. 'Love' (*agapē*) indicates the sort of concern which God has for man (1 Th. 1.4), a love grounded in the subject rather than the object and therefore independent of any quality of loveworthiness or deserving. Paul maintains that the sort of life which is appropriate to the man of faith is a life in which this love is displayed towards others ('to one another and to all men', 1 Th. 3.12), not in a vague or theoretical way but in practical and positive action: in consideration for one's fellows in matters of morality (1 Th. 4.4ff.), in responsible labour whereby one does not unnecessarily burden one's fellows nor impose on their generosity, nor encourage an opportunity for idle gossip or busybodying (1 Th. 4.9ff.; 2 Th. 3.7ff.), and even in rebukes and discipline of a right kind (2 Th. 3.15) which serve towards the ultimate wellbeing of others (2 Th. 3.6ff.). Such love works itself out in the sphere of church organization in terms of respect for those who minister (1 Th. 5.12f.), in corporate responsibility towards one another and in a general atmosphere of peace and patience (1 Th. 5.14ff.). The situation is complicated and made particularly difficult by the fact that this love has to be worked out in a hostile world amidst afflictions and trials which are both part of the Christian's lot (1 Th. 3.3f.; 2 Th. 1.5f.) and also play a part in the process of sanctification (1 Th. 3.12f.; 2 Th. 1.5). Love and patience are therefore bound inseparably together (2 Th. 3.5). Such love, worked out in ethical obedience and responsibility in the midst of hardships, is not only the proper counterpart of faith and hope, but serves the worthwhile evangelistic purpose of commanding the respect of the outsider (1 Th. 4.12).

4. ANALYSIS OF THE FIRST LETTER OF PAUL TO THE THESSALONIANS

Addresses, 1:1.
The Gospel brought to Thessalonica, 1.2–2.16.

Paul's concern for the Thessalonians, 2.17–3.13.

Instruction in Christian faith and life, 4.1–5.22.

Conclusion, 5.23–28.

5. ANALYSIS OF THE SECOND LETTER OF PAUL TO THE THESSALONIANS

Address, 1.1–2.
Perseverance in affliction, 1.3–12.

The mystery of lawlessness, 2.1–17.

Instruction in Christian faith and life, 3.1–15.

Conclusion, 3.16–18.

THE FIRST LETTER OF PAUL TO THE

THESSALONIANS

THESSALONIANS

1 Paul, Silva'nus, and Timothy,
    To the church of the Thessalo'nians in God the Father and the
Lord Jesus Christ:
    Grace to you and peace.

THE ADDRESS 1.1

1. The entire address is remarkable for its brevity. Generally at this point in a letter Paul mentions his apostleship: often he describes himself in the opening of a letter as 'servant of Jesus Christ'. The omission of apostleship here might be due to special circumstances (e.g. the existence of particularly cordial relations with the Thessalonians) or, more probably, is simply a matter of style.

Paul: Paul is to be regarded as the real author of these two epistles, though he associates with himself Silvanus and Timothy. The contents and style are Pauline and the lapses into the first person singular (in 2.18; 3.5f.; 5.27) indicate an individual rather than a corporate work. The personal salutation in 2 Th. 3.17 does not mean that the remainder of these letters is not from Paul but simply tells us that he used an amanuensis—as appears to have been his custom (cf. 1 C. 16.21; Gal. 6.11; Col. 4.18; contrast Phm. 19. In Rom. 16.22 the amanuensis himself adds a greeting).

Silvanus: the Latinized form of Silas, often mentioned in The Acts as a companion of Paul (e.g. Ac. 15.22, 40; 16.25ff.). From 2 C. 1.19 we know that he and Timothy were present with Paul in Corinth at the time this letter was written (see Introduction, pp. 3–4). Whether the Silvanus of 1 Pet. 5.12 is to be identified with Paul's companion is an open question.

Timothy: we learn from Ac. 16.1ff. that this son of a Jewish mother and Greek father joined Paul and Silvanus when they arrived at Lystra, his home town, on Paul's second missionary journey. It appears from various references to him (1 C. 16.10; Phil. 2.22) that he was young or timid, or both.

to the church: this terse address continues the brevity of the opening phrase and, as with that, is best understood simply as a matter of style (though some suggest that in his later letters Paul was consciously addressing more the church throughout the world than, as here, the local community). The LXX uses the word *ekklēsia* to translate two Hebrew words, one stemming from a root meaning 'to appoint' and the other from a root 'to call'. The early Christians thought of themselves as

the called of God, the inheritors of the divine promises. So they adopted the term
ekklēsia to describe their fellowship. In the New Testament the word describes
both the local community (at Jerusalem, Ac. 5.11; at Caesarea, Ac. 18.22, etc.)
and also the whole company of Christian communities which together comprised
(and even in their individuality represented) the people of God (cf. Rom. 16.16;
1 C. 7.17; etc.). Here Paul is using the singular and is addressing the community
of God's people in Thessalonica.

the Thessalonians: see Introduction, pp. 4–5.

in God the Father: this expression is found in Paul only here and in 2 Th. 1.2,
but no special significance should be attached to this since in his letters Paul makes
use of considerable variation in the actual form of address (cf. Rom. 1.7; 1 C. 1.2;
2 C. 1.1; etc.). The expression of an essential unity between the Father and the Son
is striking and important (see also under 3.11). In every ascription Paul is concerned
to emphasize the peculiarity of the Christian community over against other
religious groupings or secular parties and factions. Here the peculiarity is affirmed
by mention of the special, close relationship of the believers to 'God the Father
and the Lord Jesus Christ'.

and the Lord Jesus Christ: the affirmation of Christ's Lordship is characteristic
for Paul and the early church as a whole. *Kurios* is the LXX representation of the
divine name (Tetragrammaton) and was also used in antiquity of pagan deities.
It was therefore specially suited to express the early church's conviction that
Christ was Lord of all. The expression 'Jesus is Lord' quickly became a technical
clause in catechetical instruction and credal confession (cf. e.g. Rom. 10.9; 1 C.
12.3; 2 C. 4.5; Phil. 2.11). 'Lord', 'Lord Jesus' and 'the (our) Lord Jesus Christ'
are all found frequently in Paul and especially in these two epistles.

The typical opening to a letter in antiquity usually expressed some pious
sentiment in favour of the addressee. This is the case here too, only Paul expresses
a specifically *Christian* prayer. The two words, grace and peace, are found in this
context in every Pauline greeting without exception.

grace: a typical epistolary greeting in Greek writing was *chairein* (Ac. 15.23,
23.26; Jas 1.1 are examples) and the word used here, *charis*, shares the same root.
It early became part of the technical vocabulary of the preacher with particular
reference to God's special care for mankind displayed and effected in the ministry
of Jesus Christ (cf. esp. Ac. 15.11; Rom. 5.15). It signifies also any gift of God,
any dispensation of his bounty (cf. Eph. 3.7; 2 C. 8.2) and can also on occasion
signify thankfulness (Lk. 6.32f.).

peace: the common Semitic greeting was (and is) *šālôm*. Unlike our word
'peace', it means not only an absence of hostilities but a positive soundness and
rightness. In the Old Testament it becomes at times virtually equivalent to the
awaited salvation (Isa. 9.6f.). In dominical sayings it has similar meaning (cf. Mk
5.34; Jn 20.19; etc.). For Paul, it characterized the new relationship achieved
through Christ (cf. Rom. 5.1; 14.17; 1 C. 7.15).

Some important MSS add here 'from God our Father and the Lord Jesus

2 We give thanks to God always for you all, constantly mentioning you in our prayers, [3] remembering before our God and Father your work of faith and labour of love and steadfastness of hope in our Lord Jesus Christ. [4] For we know, brethren beloved by God, that he has chosen you; [5] for our gospel came to you not only

---

Christ'. Probably this arose in transmission through a knowledge of the same expression in the second epistle.

THE GOSPEL BROUGHT TO THESSALONICA 1.2–2.16

THANKSGIVING FOR THE THESSALONIAN CONVERTS 1.2–3

It is typical of Paul that he opens with a prayer of thanksgiving such as this (cf. Rom. 1.8; 1 C. 1.4; Phil. 1.3; etc. Contrast Gal. 1.6!).

2. We give thanks: the Greek verb here shares the same root as the word translated 'grace' in verse 1. It is regularly used by Paul to signify gratitude to God. Considering the haste with which Paul and his companions had left Thessalonica and the difficulties which had been encountered afterwards at Beroea, Athens, and Corinth, Paul was understandably overjoyed to receive the report from Timothy that his converts at Thessalonica were persevering in faith and love.

constantly: is taken by RSV in connection with the words in the Greek text preceding it and this is perhaps better than taking it, as in the RV, with what follows, though the sense is, in any case, not affected.

mentioning: the present participle conveys the idea of repeated regular activity. See on 'remembering' in verse 3, below.

you: is not actually in the text (save in a few MSS) but must be supplied, as in RSV, RV, etc., to be grammatical.

in our prayers: the New Testament knows two words for 'to pray' and 'prayer': the one used here, *proseuchē*, and the one which occurs in 3.10, *deēsis*. The difference in nuance is not always maintained by Paul, but basically the former word refers to prayer in general, devotion to God in prayer, whilst the other word marks specific requests made in prayers (cf. Rom. 1.10; 1 Th. 3.10; though Phil. 1.4, for example, uses *deēsis* in a general sense).

3. remembering: the verb (*mnēmoneuō*) regularly means to call something to mind or to make mention of it. In the Old Testament to remember someone or omething is very closely bound up with affecting that person or thing—so, e.g., n Mal. 4.4 'remember the law' means in effect 'take note of and obey . . .'. So here, the sense is that Paul calls to mind the Thessalonians' condition not only in a vague way but in the concrete and effective sense of praying for them.

before our God and Father: RSV (and NEB) takes this expression in conjunction with 'remembering'. Grammatically, in the Greek, it can mean that Paul remembers before God the Thessalonians' activity, or that the Thessalonians' work and labour takes place before God: both would make good sense. Possibly it is best to allow, as RV does by leaving the expression to the end, a certain ambiguity.

Paul specifies three matters about which he is thankful:

your work of faith: Paul's belief that salvation was to be accepted through faith did not mean that faith was an idle thing. The faith which appropriates salvation authenticates itself as *real* faith, conviction, and commitment, through responsible and serious action (so cf. here chapters 4–5). 'Faith', for Paul, hardly ever means simply 'faithfulness', but on the other hand faithfulness is hardly ever absent from the idea of faith.

The three phrases used here have the same form, a noun followed by a descriptive genitive serving as a strong adjective. Paul means work prompted and characterized by faith, labour prompted and characterized by love, and steadfastness prompted and characterized by hope.

and labour of love: the Greek word *kopos*, over against the more frequent New Testament word for work *ergon*, denotes arduous, wearying toil involving sweat and fatigue (cf. especially 2 C. 6.5; 2 Th. 3.8). 'Love' here translates the Greek *agapē*. In the New Testament there are two words for love (Greek had a third, *erōs*, which does not occur in the New Testament). *Agapē*, little used in Greek until taken into the Christian vocabulary, is used specifically of God's love for, apart from and independent of, man. This love is grounded in God's own nature (Jn 3.16; Rom. 5.8) and is displayed and made effective supremely in Jesus Christ and the events of his life, death and resurrection. This love prompts into being love *for* God (Rom. 5.5) and love for one's fellows, especially one's fellow Christians (1 Th. 3.12; 1 Jn 4.20f.). The other word, *philia*, is in comparison little used and is often synonymous with *agapē*.

steadfastness of hope: the third object of Paul's thankfulness is the patient endurance characterized by hope which the Thessalonians have evinced. Patience, *hupomonē*, is a typically Pauline word: he can speak of the 'God of patience' (Rom. 15.5), of his own patience (2 C. 6.4), as well as the patience of others. It is never in Paul mere optimism nor passive resignation, but is active and positive. Here it is expressly linked with hope, and almost certainly the hope signified is hope in the Parousia of Christ when all that is in store for the Christian and the world will be revealed (cf. 1 Pet. 1.5). This is true whether the phrase 'in our Lord Jesus Christ' is understood with this expression (as Findlay, Milligan and others suggest) or not. Christian hope is grounded upon Christ's resurrection (1 Pet. 1.3; 1 C. 15.12ff.) and focused upon his return (1 Pet. 1.13). The early church was sharply distinguished from its pagan neighbours by its intense hope, for the world of ancient Greek and Roman times was, despite its achievement and glories, pathetically hopeless (cf. C. E. B. Cranfield, *I and II Peter*, pp. 36f.).

in our Lord Jesus Christ: grammatically this can be taken with the last of the three previous phrases or with all three together, and the latter alternative is preferable because for Paul, faith, love, and hope all spring from fellowship with Christ and have him as their object. This is the first occasion of many where we find this triplet (cf. Rom. 5.2ff.; Gal. 5.5f.; Col. 1.4f.; Heb.6.10ff.; 1 Pet. 1.21f.; and especially 1 C. 13.13). It may be that Paul has adopted an existing Christian practice in bringing the three ideas together.

THE GOSPEL PROCLAIMED IN THESSALONICA 1.4–10

4. For we know: RSV wisely often translates participles by indicatives, and does so here.

brethren: Paul's favourite word for his fellow-Christians is 'brethren', used very often throughout the epistles but proportionately more in Thessalonians (twenty-one times) than elsewhere.

beloved by God: not often does Paul strengthen the term 'brethren' with 'beloved' (cf. 1 C. 15.58), though he often uses 'beloved' instead of 'brethren.' Here (as also in Rom. 1.7) the brethren are beloved *of God* (AV wrongly took 'of God' in connection with 'election'), but unlike Rom. 1.7 (and similar to Jude 1) Paul uses the perfect participle, suggesting a decisive past event as well as a continuing reality.

that he has chosen you: the Greek has literally 'your election', but RSV rightly interprets this. Paul generally is content to speak of calling (*kaleomai*) and election (*eklegō*) in a rather unsystematic way (he offers something of a scheme of salvation in Rom. 8.28ff., and grapples with the problems presented by disbelieving Israel in Rom. 9–11). Usually he thinks of the 'called' and the 'chosen' as synonymous (contrast Mt. 22.14). Clearly Paul sets before us an unsolved mystery in speaking of election, and in grappling with this matter it is important to recognize (1) that God's election somehow centres upon Jesus Christ (see J. K. S. Reid, 'Determinate', in *A Theological Word Book of the Bible*, ed. Richardson, London, 1950, pp. 64ff.), and (2) that it is closely connected in Paul's thought not with God's arbitrariness nor with his anger, but with his love (as in this verse). Paul claims to recognize the election of his converts in Thessalonica by their positive response to the gospel.

5. Election is something which stems from God, but it involves definite human action, especially preaching and the response of faith. Paul now writes of these.

for our gospel: the word *euangelion* was used in Roman times to refer to the glad announcement of the birth of an heir to the throne, of the accession of a new emperor and similar important events. But to understand its use here and throughout the New Testament it is essential to recognize its Old Testament background. The LXX uses *euangelizō* to translate a Hebrew verb meaning to announce good news, especially the good news of God's salvation, the advent of his reign (cf. especially Isa. 40.9, 41.27, 52.7, 60.6). Apparently without strict differentiation Paul speaks of 'my gospel' (Rom. 2.16, 16.25), of 'our' gospel (as here), and of 'the gospel of God' (Rom. 1.1, 15.16 and cf. some MSS of this verse) or 'of Christ' (3.2, Rom. 1.16; 2 C. 9.13; etc.). Clearly 'our' is only very loosely possessive, to be understood as 'the gospel we preached' (as in 2.9). Paul is here

in word, but also in power and in the Holy Spirit and with full
conviction. You know what kind of men we proved to be among
you for your sake. ⁶ And you became imitators of us and of the Lord,

---

looking back to the time when he had first proclaimed the good news to the
Thessalonians that God's kingly rule had been revealed in Jesus Christ.

came to you: Paul thinks of the gospel as something real and vital so that it is
not only 'preached' but 'comes'. This thought is now expanded.

not only in word . . . : the contrast is between the mere presentation of a message
and an effective, dynamic proclamation (cf. the similar contrast in 1 C. 2.4, 4.20).
But Paul does not mean that his preaching was effective on account of some skill
with words: 2.3ff. seems to denounce the sort of pleasing speech to which men
willingly listen and to which Paul's contemporaries were quite accustomed (cf.
especially 1 C. 2.1). Rather, the message was effective because of *God's* power
working through the spoken word (*dunamis*, the Greek word for power is
generally used by Paul of divine energy). Hence Paul here expands the thought
by adding 'and in the Holy Spirit', by which phrase he draws special attention to
the early church's conviction that its mission was directed and furthered by God
through his Spirit (for the Spirit mediates Christ to the believer, Jn 14.26; etc.,
he also mediates Christ through believers to those outside, Ac. 5.32, and he even
directs the geographical development of the mission, Ac. 13.2, 16.6f.).

and with full conviction: the same word (*plērophoria*) occurs in Col. 2.2
where it refers to a certain maturity of understanding and conviction. Here it
means the sure response of faith indicative of and arising from the power of
God's Spirit.

You know: in the Greek the next clause is introduced by the particle *kathōs*,
'as' or 'according as', suggesting more than the RSV does that the clause balances
verses 4–5a ('we know . . . as you know'). As the apostle recalls the converts'
response of faith, of which he was witness, he reminds them that they also can
recall how the missionaries behaved towards them. The verse preludes the further
treatment of the matter in 2.1–12.

A theme of these letters is that the Thessalonians already know the essentials of
Christian faith and life (cf. 2.1, 5, 10, 11; 3.3, 4; 4.2; 5.2; and also 2 Th. 2.5, 6,
15; 3.7).

for your sake: cf. 1 C. 4.6; 2 C. 4.15; 8.9 and Phil. 1.24.

6. and you became imitators of us and of the Lord: Paul has no false
modesty! The Greek word 'imitators' (*mimētai*) is found in the New Testament
only in Paul and Hebrews. To the Corinthians he writes 'be ye imitators of me'
(1 C. 4.16) but, as the same letter makes explicit, he wishes this only because he
himself is an imitator of Christ (1 C. 11.1). So here the imitation is of the
missionaries *and* of the Lord. (We may compare 2.14, which speaks of 'imitators

for you received the word in much affliction, with joy inspired by
the Holy Spirit; ⁷ so that you became an example to all the believers
in Macedo'nia and in Acha'ia. ⁸ For not only has the word of the
Lord sounded forth from you in Macedo'nia and Acha'ia, but your
faith in God has gone forth everywhere, so that we need not say

---

of the churches of God' and Eph. 5.1, where we read 'imitators of God'.) The
word *mimētai* certainly expresses more than the AV rendering 'followers'.

for you received the word: the expression 'to receive' (the word, or the gospel)
quickly became almost a technical term for the acceptance of the faith: for this
the usual word is *paralambanō* (see below on 2.13). The word used here, *dechomai*,
generally has the nuance 'to welcome' as one would a guest (cf. Gal. 4.14). 'The
word' signifies the whole gospel message. *Logos*, the Greek word used here, occurs
more than three hundred times in the New Testament. In verse 5 it expressed a
contrast between mere speaking and effective preaching. Here it is short-hand for
'the word of God' (cf. e.g. Rom. 9.6; I C. 14.36, where Paul uses the complete
phrase). It is the New Testament equivalent of the Old Testament 'the word of
the Lord' (which occurs over four hundred times) and carries the same significance
of power and effectiveness (cf. Isa. 55.11 and the 'power' mentioned above in
verse 5 which accompanies the preaching of God's word). In this epistle Paul uses
without differentiation 'the word', 'the word of God' (2.13) and 'the word of the
Lord' (1.8).

in much affliction: *Thlipsis*, the Greek word here, occurs twenty-four times in
Paul (forty-five times in the whole New Testament). In the LXX it is used
frequently to describe the innocent suffering of the just. For Paul, the word
describes the certain expectation and inevitable character of the Christian life. It
carries also eschatological significance, tribulation being (as also in Judaism) a sign
of the End (though whereas in Judaism it was awaited, for Paul it was already
present: see further on 2 Th. 2.3ff.).

The affliction referred to here was, if Ac. 17.1ff. is to be believed, caused by
Jewish malevolence. Being moved with jealousy, they caused a civic uproar and
took some of the new converts before the authorities charging them with sedition
(see further, Introduction p. 3).

with joy inspired by the Holy Spirit: cf. Rom. 14.17; Gal. 5.22. The Greek
simply has 'joy of the Holy Spirit', but RSV is quite right in understanding this
joy as 'inspired' by the Spirit (it is the Greek genitive of origin). The paradox of
affliction borne with joy is explained in this way: it is not stoicism nor foolhardi-
ness, but the working of God. 'Joy', like tribulation, has for Paul eschatological
overtones, for it belongs most properly to the End and is possible only because of
the advent of Christ and the outpouring of the Spirit.

7. The writer's thought moves on from the conversion of the Thessalonians to

their subsequent influence upon fellow-believers. As they had 'imitated' the
apostles, so they became in turn a 'pattern' for others to follow.

an example: *Tupos*, the word used here, could mean an impression made by a
seal or some other object (cf. Jn 20.25 'the print' of the nails), the imprint on a coin,
a statue or image, and thence a model, type or image in the abstract sense. Paul
uses it in Phil. 3.17 and 2 Th. 3.9 of examples to follow, and in 1 C. 10.6 of
examples to avoid.

Presumably the Thessalonians' joyous acceptance of affliction encouraged other
Christian communities and individuals.

in Macedonia and in Achaia: the two provinces which together comprised
the whole of Greece. In these provinces Paul established Christian communities
during his second missionary journey (Ac. 16.9–17.14), visiting them again in the
course of his third journey (Ac. 20.1ff.). There cannot at this time have been very
great numbers of Christians, particularly in the regions beyond the towns visited
(Philippi, Beroea, etc.), but Paul naturally thinks in terms of provinces, and one
should not underestimate the speed and facility of communication in the Roman
Empire.

8. The thought of verse 7 is now repeated and expanded. Not only have the
Thessalonians set an example of joyful endurance of trials, but also from them the
gospel has been passed on to others all over the place.

sounded forth: the Greek *exechetai* is found only here in the New Testament,
though it occurs in the LXX. (Cognate words are found in 1 C. 13.1 'sounding
brass'; Ac. 2.2 'the sound' from heaven; a 'sound of a trumpet'; and Lk. 4.37,
translated in RSV 'reports'.) It is an expressive word suggesting an echoing like
thunder or sounding out as a trumpet. The verb is in the perfect tense (which
occurs in the New Testament only infrequently). The translation suggesting
something finished does not convey what the Greek perfect intends, namely the
idea of a result continuing into the present.

your faith in God: synonymous with 'receiving the word' in verse 6. What
Paul considers to be involved in faith he explains in verses 9–10. Sometimes Paul
means by faith the subjective quality of faithfulness or the experience of commitment to the gospel (cf. e.g. Rom. 1.8; Eph. 1.15) and sometimes the objective
events which together comprise the gospel (cf. e.g. Gal. 1.23; 1 C. 16.13). In
many cases, and particularly here, he may well have had both aspects in mind.

has gone forth: another perfect tense, again indicating continuing repercussions.

everywhere: lit. in every place. There may be slight exaggeration here: on the
other hand, once the churches had been established in these provinces it would not
be long before word of them would travel out in all directions.

we need not say anything: verses 9–10 show that the Thessalonians' faith had
been correctly understood of others and that for Paul to have spoken further about
it would have been superfluous. (The Greek for 'say' here is *lalein*, which refers
to the act of speaking; the other New Testament word, *legein*, refers more to the
message being spoken.)

anything. ⁹ For they themselves report concerning us what a welcome we had among you, and how you turned to God from idols, to serve a living and true God, ¹⁰ and to wait for his Son from heaven, whom he raised from the dead, Jesus who delivers us from the wrath to come.

---

9. They themselves: i.e. people generally.

report: an unusual word (*apangellō*) for Paul, found only here and in 1 C. 14.25. In common Greek it had lost its special emphasis, but here (and in 1 C. 14.25) it retains its note of serious declaration.

concerning us: the interchange of 'you' and 'we' runs throughout. The missionaries' behaviour has already been mentioned in verse 5 and will be taken up much more fully in 2.1–12. This is not mere selfconsciousness but the conviction that in the progress of the gospel missionary and convert are bound very much together (hence, too, the exhortation in 5.25).

welcome: the Greek (*eisodos*) is really neutral, like our word 'reception'. That the missionaries were *gladly* received appears from what follows rather than from the word used here. (RV is more accurate in its 'entering in'.)

What follows is a summary account of the events which comprised the conversion of the Thessalonians. Paul mentions three factors: (1) turning from idols: (2) turning to the living God: (3) waiting for his Son from heaven. The vocabulary here is not typically Pauline and it may well be that we have here primitive missionary tradition.

you turned to God: the more usual New Testament word for turning from sin towards God is *metanoeō*. Here Paul uses *epistrephō* (elsewhere only in 2 C. 3.16 and Gal. 4.9), but with the same significance.

from idols: Paul means all heathenism, all worship which is not directed towards the true God. 'Idols' embraces not only the artistic representations of gods but the reality supposed to exist behind them: Paul maintains that there is no reality behind them (cf. 1 C. 8.4 'an idol has no real existence'), though to worship idols is to be in league with the devil (1 C. 10.20f.).

to serve a living and true God: this is the second factor in conversion. The Greek word translated 'to serve' means literally to serve as a slave. For Paul there is no real freedom in this world: worship of idols means bondage to sin (Rom. 6.20), and worship of the true God means to be his 'slave' (Paul habitually calls himself the slave of Jesus Christ). Paradoxically, it is in this bondage to the living God that the only possibility of freedom is to be found (cf. Gal. 4.7, and with it 1 Pet. 2.16).

Over against idols, God is 'living' and 'true'. Together these words emphasize his reality and genuineness over against the insubstantial, shadowy and non-existent 'gods' of the heathen.

10. and to wait for his Son: the third factor in the Thessalonians' conversion is their hope. Their stance is one of waiting (*anamenō* found only here in the New Testament again suggests perhaps a pre-Pauline missionary tradition). The object of their hope is the second advent, the Parousia of Christ. Some modern scholars maintain that the idea of a return of Christ at the end of time was foreign to Jesus' thought and lacking in the earliest Christian preaching and confessions (cf. esp. Glasson, pp. 63ff., and Robinson, pp. 22ff.). The advent hope arose, they suggest, through transference of Old Testament theophanic imagery to Christ (Glasson) or to an unreconciled confusion of christologies (Robinson). These explanations seem particularly weak. The transference of Old Testament references to Jesus on the basis of the conviction that 'Jesus is Lord' is difficult because the gospels speak particularly of a Parousia of the *Son of Man*. And the evidence for a supposed confusion of christologies, Acts 2 and 3, is patient of interpretations other than that of Bishop Robinson. Furthermore, that the Parousia hope did not form part of the content of the earliest 'conversion' preaching is understandable for that preaching (if the early speeches in The Acts can be relied on) called for repentance and faith on the basis of *past* events, specifically the death and resurrection of Christ. Hope in the Parousia was expressed, in the first place, not in preaching but in prayer (cf. 'our Lord come' in 1 C. 16.22; Rev. 22.20; Did. 10.6), and in the attitude of 'waiting' of which Paul speaks here. It seems to the present writer that the evidence for the presence both in Jesus' teaching and in the life of the early church of a Parousia expectation can be denied only if recourse is had to serious and unwarranted textual surgery (see further O. Cullmann, *Christ and Time*).

his Son: the only occurrence in these epistles of this phrase (also absent from Phil., Col. and Phm.).

from heaven: lit. from the heavens. Some have explained the plural as a Semitism, but Paul employs the singular (ten times) almost as often as the plural (eleven times) apparently without significance unless perhaps to give, through the plural, extra solemnity to what he is saying. The expression reminds us of passages such as Mk 13.26 par. Christ would naturally return 'from heaven' since it was 'into heaven' that he had ascended (Ac. 1.9f.; 3.20f.).

whom he raised from the dead: great weight was laid in early Christian preaching on the cross of Christ (cf. e.g. 1 C. 2.2), but the central feature was his resurrection, of which the apostles were witnesses (as Ac. 1.22; 2.32; 3.15; etc.; 1 C. 15.4ff. testify). Paul was convinced that his preaching and his converts' faith had to stand or fall according as to whether this resurrection had happened or not (1 C. 15.14). The resurrection was, according to Paul, God's act (here, as throughout the New Testament it is *God* who raises his Son) vindicating Christ's death and containing the assurance of his victory over the dominion of sin and death (Rom. 6.9).

Jesus: Paul does not often use this single personal name (only some fifteen times

T.C.B.: T.—2*

2 For you yourselves know, brethren, that our visit to you was not in vain; ² but though we had already suffered and been shamefully treated at Philippi, as you know, we had courage in our God to declare to you the gospel of God in the face of great opposition. ³ For our appeal does not spring from error or

---

in all his letters). Here, having spoken of the 'Son', he identifies him as 'Jesus'. (For the significance of this name see V. Taylor, *The Names of Jesus*, pp. 5-11.)

who delivers us: the Greek *rhuomenon*, is a present participle, indicating a lasting function. In classical Greek and in the LXX it means 'to rescue', 'redeem', 'save', and suggests perhaps more than RSV 'deliver' the avoidance of great danger.

from the wrath to come: Jewish expectation included the belief that God would one day openly and finally inflict punishment upon all that was contrary to his rule (cf. e.g. Ps. 79.6; Hos. 5.10). This expectation continues in the New Testament, though, like every aspect of prior expectation, it now centres upon Jesus Christ. Hence Paul maintains here that *he*, Jesus, is the one who can deliver from the wrath that is to come: similarly he, Jesus, is the one through whom God's wrath will be revealed (2 Th. 1.7f.).

to come: the Greek again has a present participle, 'coming', which serves well to suggest that the wrath which is definitely in the future (cf. Rom. 2.5, 8; 5.9) is proleptically present and active (1 Th. 2.7; Rom. 1.18). There is always a certain tension when Paul speaks of deliverance or of wrath for, in one sense, he believed that God had already in Jesus Christ enacted his wrath and his merciful deliverance: already men could participate in this deliverance and this wrath through faith, or lack of it: but because the deliverance and the wrath were enacted in a strange, unexpected and hidden way in the person and work of Jesus, Paul still awaited a final, open declaration of this deliverance and wrath in the final and open manifestation of Jesus himself (see further on 2.12).

The Manner in which the Gospel was Proclaimed 2.1-12

1. The apostle's thought returns to 1.5 and 9. His defence of his conduct at Thessalonica at some length here suggests that the Jewish opponents who had, according to Ac. 17, stirred up trouble for the Christians, or the pagan civic authorities, or both, were attempting to slander the missionaries in their absence (see Introduction p. 3).

you yourselves know: this balances the 'they themselves report' of 1.9. The emphatic form of the Greek here seems to imply some slanderous suggestion of impure motives.

our visit: the same Greek noun is used here as in 1.9, translated 'welcome', emphasizing the link with that verse.

was not in vain: the word for vain (*kenos*) has two meanings in Greek, both of which are found in the New Testament. The primary meaning is 'void', 'empty', 'a mere nothing' (Mk 12.3 uses it meaning empty-handed). The other meaning, derived from this, is 'ineffective', 'without result' (cf. 1 C. 15.58). There is some question which meaning Paul intended here. In favour of the second meaning we note (1) that elsewhere Paul uses *kenos*, meaning fruitless and worthless (cf. 1 C. 15.10, 14, 58; Gal. 2.2; Eph. 5.6; Phil. 2.6 (possibly); Col. 2.8; 1 Th. 3.5). (2) That Paul lays great weight on the results of his mission at Thessalonica. (3) That to point to an effective and lasting result of his work would be an effective answer to the charge of being a charlatan. In favour of the former meaning we note (1) that the word *can* have this meaning and perhaps does in Phil. 2.6. (2) That Paul immediately recounts how he brought the gospel to the Thessalonians at great cost to himself (verse 2), even working all hours of the day and night to avoid being a burden to his converts (verse 9), meaning that he did not come empty-handed but with much to offer. (3) That this would be a fitting argument against a charge of extortion. We cannot be sure which meaning Paul intended, and indeed he may have chosen this ambiguity.

2. but: the Greek work here (*alla*) indicates an emphatic contrast.

suffered and been shamefully treated: *Propaschein* is the word translated 'suffered', and it occurs only here in the New Testament, though in its simpler form (*paschein*) it is found frequently: it denotes pain, generally physical (see further on 2.15). The word rendered 'shamefully treated' is also rare in the New Testament and only here in Paul. It means to outrage, affront, or insult. The suffering meant is what happened at Philippi. There, according to Ac. 16.19ff., Paul and Silas were beaten with rods, imprisoned and fastened in the stocks. Public flogging of a Roman citizen was certainly an outrage (Ac. 16.38), which naturally added to the physical pain involved (cf. Paul's outburst of indignation in Ac. 16.37).

at Philippi: according to Ac. 17.1 Paul had come directly from Philippi along the Via Egnatia to Thessalonica.

we had courage: the Greek here is a composite verb basically meaning 'having all speech' and it was used in classical Greek to signify freedom of speech or expression, often with a political connotation. So here Paul means something like 'we had complete freedom of speech' (cf. Moffatt's, 'we took courage and confidence', or NEB 'frankly and fearlessly').

our God: the phrase occurs again in 3.9 and 2 Th. 1.11, 12. NEB 'by the help of our God' gives the sense intended. Perhaps Paul knew the saying of Mk 13.11 and had this in mind as he recounts the way the missionaries preached under difficult circumstances.

the gospel of God: cf. on 1.5. We may compare the phrase in Mk 1.1 'the gospel of Jesus Christ', where, as here, the genitive is best understood both as subjective and as objective.

in the face of great opposition: lit. 'in much conflict', though the Greek *agōn* could mean as well 'fight', 'contention' or a 'race'. It is possible that Paul meant

uncleanness, nor is it made with guile; ⁴ but just as we have been approved by God to be entrusted with the gospel, so we speak, not to please men, but to please God who tests our hearts. ⁵ For we never

---

the inward agony and mental struggle to go on preaching despite the 'suffering and shameful treatment' (as Frame suggests). More probably he meant the speedy opposition aroused by his preaching at Thessalonica which led to his hasty departure (see Introduction p. 3). Perhaps, again, Paul recognized and intended a certain ambiguity in the expression.

3. The writer now enters into details concerning the mission at Thessalonica, reminding his converts of the purity and uprightness of the missionaries' motives and behaviour. As we read the various defences offered, we can guess at the sort of charges being levelled against Paul and his companions by the troublemakers.

our appeal: the same word used here can mean 'comfort' (as in Ac. 9.31), but Paul uses it to mean 'exhortation' almost as one might speak of a sermon as an exhortation (as in Ac. 13.15). He means more than his manner of preaching: 'appeal' means the whole enterprise of preaching as it was directed towards winning converts to the faith.

does not spring: there is nothing in the Greek here. Paul simply says, 'our appeal . . . not from error', but clearly RSV supplies the sense intended. The tense is certainly present (cf. verse 4) suggesting that Paul is referring not only to the Thessalonian mission but also to preaching in general.

from error: Paul maintains that his message was free from three different impurities, error, uncleanness, and guile. Error, *planē*, comes again in 2 Th. 2.11.

uncleanness: in the ancient world moral standards tended to be extremely low, and in many religious cults ritual prostitution was rife. Christian preaching, says Paul, has no dealings with such impurities.

nor is it made with guile: again there is no verb in the Greek but RSV rightly distinguishes between the first two phrases introduced by the Greek *ek*, 'from' or 'springing from', and this one constructed with the Greek *en*, 'in' or 'in an atmosphere of'. The first two phrases speak of origin, this third of manner. The word 'guile', *dolos*, means in classical Greek a bait or trap (in this sense it comes in Mt. 26.24) and thence any form of trick or stratagem. 2 C. 12.16 shows that Paul was accused of crafty trickery at Corinth. He holds that there was never any atmosphere of deceit about his preaching.

From these phrases it appears that in general terms Paul and his associates were accused by their opponents of being preachers of wrong ideas, practicers of immoral behaviour, and purveyors of an atmosphere of black magic. Roving preachers and charlatans of that sort were frequent spectacles in the world of the time, and Paul takes the charges seriously.

4. but: another strong adversative (cf. verse 2). Contrary to the charges behind verse 3, the missionaries have been approved by God for their work, their message is entrusted to them by him and their chief concern is to please him in their preaching.

as we have been approved: the word means to scrutinize, and as a result to approve and entrust. The tense in the Greek is perfect, indicating a lasting approval and not something over and done with. (For Paul's sense of this divine approval, cf. 1 C. 4.1–5.)

entrusted: having been approved, they were entrusted. The idea of the derivative nature of the gospel clearly qualifies the possessive 'our gospel' in 1.5, etc. Paul accounted himself to be completely at the disposal of the gospel and its progress (1 C. 9.13, 23).

so we speak: the present tense (as before) indicates that Paul is enunciating a general principle for all his preaching and not just explaining what happened at Thessalonica.

not to please men: the Greek word here translated 'please' is found in inscriptions of people who have served their fellow citizens or 'the common good'. It means considerably more than 'give pleasure to', conveying the sense of service and obedience (the same word is used in verse 15 of the Jews, who by their rejection of Christ 'displease' God). Here the meaning is patently not that Paul is careless of the common good: rather, his *chief* concern is serving and obeying God. His mission is not to serve the whim or fancy or even supposed needs of his fellows— though, actually, by obeying God he would certainly have claimed to have been serving the best interests of his fellows too.

but to please God: the Greek does not repeat the verb but in English it is better (with RSV) to do so. 'To please God' is Paul's summary of the Christian attitude of dependence and service. The thought throughout is very close to 1 C. 4.1–5 (and cf. Ac. 2.19).

who tests our hearts: 'tests' is the same verb (*dokimazō*) as was translated earlier in the verse by 'approved'. The scrutiny and consequent approval is a continuous process. (Paul expresses awareness of this constant testing most strikingly in 1 C. 9.27.) The play on words in the Greek is reproduced by Moffatt with his 'attests . . . tests'. The phrase used here is not infrequent in the Old Testament (cf. 1 Chr. 29.17; Ps. 7.9; Prov. 17.3; Jer. 11.20, etc.).

hearts: in the Old Testament 'heart' means variously the inner man (in contrast to some outward feature of man: cf. Dt. 30.14; Ezek. 3.10), man in his capacity to reflect and consider (e.g. Dt. 8.5), man's moral character (e.g. Dt. 9.5, 10.16) and thence his conscience (Job 27.6), the seat of man's emotions (e.g. Isa. 30.29) or man as he converses within himself (Dt. 7.17; Isa. 14.13). Paul was familiar with this usage and widens the usual Greek meaning of *kardia*, heart, in company with the other New Testament writers, to include similar senses.

5. Paul goes now into more details concerning his behaviour at Thessalonica. As, in verse 3, he listed three vices from which his preaching in general was free, so now he lists three forms of corruption from which his preaching at Thessalonica

used either words of flattery, as you know, or a cloak for greed, as God is witness; [6] nor did we seek glory from men, whether from you or from others, though we might have made demands as apostles of Christ. [7] But we were gentle among you, like a nurse

---

in particular had been free (verses 5–6). They are, flattery, greed, and self-seeking.

words of flattery: lit. 'we were never in word of flattery', but the sense is clear. Flattery here means not the harmless exaggeration or nice compliment but something akin to 'currying favour', deception by slick eloquence, the idea being to win over the hearers in order to exploit them.

as you know: cf. 1.5 and 2.2.

a cloak for greed: the Greek word 'cloak' (*prophasis*) mostly has a bad sense about it. It can mean the apparent cause of something, generally suggesting a true cause to which it is opposed: or, more simply, it can mean a mere excuse, a pretext. Paul uses it in Phil. 1.18, meaning 'insincere and hypocritical'. Here Paul indicates that his preaching of the faith was undertaken with the sincere motive of pleasing God and of offering his hearers the gospel, not with any underhand pretext of gaining something for himself. Just what he might have sought, had he been insincere, is contained in the word 'greed' (*pleonexia*), which in classical Greek and in the New Testament means considerably more than desire for money: it embraces the sense of arrogant self-assertion and aggrandisement which often lies behind greediness for money. Paul not infrequently connects it closely with uncleanness (Rom. 1.29; Eph. 5.3; Col. 3.5). The word here is in the genitive, having the function of a strong adjective (cf. on 1.3).

as God is witness: from calling upon the Thessalonian converts to witness to the truth of what he is saying ('you know' in 1.5, 2.2 and this verse) Paul turns to God as witness to his sincerity and honesty. (cf. similarly Rom. 1.9; 2 C. 1.23 and verse 10 of this chapter.)

6. The third form of corruption from which Paul says his preaching at Thessalonica was free is personal aggrandisement and praise.

seek: Paul is careful not to mention what he did or did not, in fact, receive, simply affirming that his *intention* was not to draw honour to himself. In a sense his converts *do* reflect to his praise (cf. 2.20 'for you are our glory and our joy'), and Paul elsewhere shows that he is not unaware of his contribution in furthering the progress of the gospel (cf. 1 C. 15.10), although he realizes that the real power is God's and the true glory God's (1 C. 15.9f.). Nevertheless, he solemnly affirms that he never sought aggrandisement for himself.

glory: the word 'glory' is used in the New Testament often of God to signify the majesty and wonder of his presence (Lk. 2.9; 21.27, etc.) but is also used, as here, in the ordinary sense of praise and merit on account of some human quality or achievement.

whether from you or from others: by 'others' Paul could mean Christians in other cities. We have already seen (1.7-10) that other churches were impressed by the Thessalonians' response. Or he could mean the others in Thessalonica as distinct from the converts there (the thought then being similar to verse 4, 'not to please men'). Probably the reference is to anyone in general.

The thought of this section is very close-knit, particularly in verses 6 and 7. The idea of seeking personal advantage (6a) leads on to the thought that as apostles of Christ some service might be due to them (6b), although this possibility was not realized (7a). There is some difference of opinion where the verse division here should be. RV, RSV and NEB read the same, but the Nestle edition of the Greek text divides after 'or from others', and some commentators favour this. In any case, the development of thought must be interpreted independently of the verse divisions (which were first made by one Stephanus for the Greek text printed in 1551).

demands: (RV 'been burdensome', with footnote alternative 'claimed honour': NEB, 'made our weight felt': Moffatt, 'men of weight'.) RSV captures the ambiguity of the Greek word used (*baros*) which, from its basic meaning 'weight', can mean a burden, i.e. the apostles could have asked for and expected their keep; or it can mean weight in the sense of importance and influence, i.e. the apostles could have expected and even demanded some honour. The second alternative might seem to follow from what Paul has just said about not seeking glory (6a): but against this view and in favour of the former alternative we notice (1) the apostle actually is nowhere in Paul's letters thought of as worthy of special honour amongst his fellows. In 1 C. 12.28f. it seems that the apostle ranks 'first' among his church officials, but 'first' in the New Testament sense means far from (almost the opposite of) chief in honour among men (cf. especially Mk 10.43-45), and it seems unlikely that Paul, the slave of Jesus Christ and the servant of men for Christ's sake (2 C. 4.5), would have regarded claiming honour as even a theoretical possibility. (2) On the other hand, the New Testament does say that the preacher is 'worthy of his hire' (Lk. 10.7), a saying no doubt known to Paul and probably referred to by him in 1 C. 9.14 (the principle is enlarged on by Paul in 1 C. 9.4ff.: cf. also 2 Th. 3.9). (3) The thought which follows in verses 7-9 supports this interpretation, for Paul is saying there that the missionaries regarded their converts as weak and needy and were far from piling burdens upon them.

apostles of Christ: the meaning of the word *apostolos* in the New Testament derives from a Hebrew Old Testament word meaning personal representative and agent. In the New Testament it is often used of the Twelve, Christ's commissioned agents (cf. Lk. 6.13 with Mk 3.14), but it is also used of a larger group of disciples (cf. Ac. 14.4; 1 C. 15.7). We simply do not know exactly what qualifications were needed for someone to be accounted an apostle in the early church, but clearly his function was to witness to Christ (hence the stress on having been an eyewitness of him, Ac. 1.21f.). The church soon came to restrict the title to the Twelve and Paul. It is sometimes noted that in 2 C. 1.1 Paul seems to avoid

taking care of her children. ⁸ So, being affectionately desirous of
you, we were ready to share with you not only the gospel of God
but also our own selves, because you had become very dear to us.

9 For you remember our labour and toil, brethren; we worked
night and day, that we might not burden any of you, while we

---

calling Timothy an apostle, but in the present verse 'apostles' most naturally refers
to all three, Paul, Silvanus and Timothy.

7. But: another (cf. 2.2 and 2.4) strong adversative. Far from having been a
burden to their converts, the apostles nurtured them.

we were gentle: there is a difficulty here because some good MSS have *ēpios*,
meaning gentle, and others (rather better) have *nēpios*, babes. The confusion could
easily have arisen since the word prior to this one ends with an 'n', and such little
scribal mistakes are not infrequent. Some commentators, seeing that 'babes'
makes rather awkward sense (and mixes the metaphors!) judge it therefore likely
to be the original which was later altered to the word that gave an easier sense.
But on the whole 'gentle' seems preferable, partly because it occurs only twice in
the New Testament and could easily have been mistaken for the more common
word 'babe', and partly because Paul usually uses 'babe' in a bad sense (1 C. 3.1,
13.11; Gal. 4.3; Eph. 4.14). Paul was kindly towards his converts, like a parent
towards his children. (The word is used in Greek of the kindness of a father:
verse 11 is to some extent anticipated in this thought.)

among you: the expression, as well as the thought, brings to mind Lk. 22.27.

like a nurse: found only here in the New Testament, this word (*trophos*) means
basically a 'feeder', and so a wet-nurse. We have a similar picture of Paul milk-
feeding his converts in 1 C. 3.1f. (and of Paul as a mother in Gal. 4.19). Far from
begging their bread, the missionaries actually 'fed' their converts!

taking care of: the word in Greek is from a root meaning warmth. Metaphorically it came to mean 'to foster', 'to nurture' (in Dt. 22.6 it is used of a bird
warming her eggs).

her children: 'her' is emphatic here, suggesting the nurse's own children whom
she looks after with special affection.

8. Being affectionately desirous of you: the Greek verb here is a *hap. leg.*
in the New Testament and is uncertain in etymology and meaning. Various
conjectures have been made about it. It is found on a grave describing the parents'
sad yearning for their dead child, and it seems to indicate deep affection and great
attraction. That Paul's affection for his converts was very great is clear from 2.17f.

we were ready: the Greek has a present indicative (which some texts have
'corrected' to imperfect), but the meaning is past, as the verbs in 7a and 8b show.
This word comes again in 3.1, where the readiness in question means almost

'making the best of the situation'. Here, however, the sense demanded is of a glad willingness.

to share with you: some scholars regard the Greek word used here (*metadidōmi*) as a synonym for the simple verb *didōmi* used with 'own self' (as here) in e.g. Mk 10.45. But the compound verb actually introduces an idea of mutuality into the giving, which RSV 'share' helps to translate. (One is reminded of the mutuality of ministry, somewhat laboriously expressed, in Rom. 1.11f.)

gospel of God: cf. verse 2.

but also our own selves: Paul means that not only did he sustain his converts by feeding them with the gospel, by which he too was sustained, but that he and his companions shared their very lives, out of love, with them. They did more than share a message, they established bonds of mutual love. 'Selves' is the Greek *psuchē*, 'soul', which in the New Testament is sometimes used of soul as opposed to body (Mt. 10.28), but generally means 'life', 'self', or, as here, 'entire being'.

you had become very dear to us: in 1.4 the Thessalonians were called 'beloved of God': here Paul says that they were beloved of the missionaries too. (RSV hides the fact that the same word is used in the Greek though with different constructions.)

9. The remembrance that he had not been a burden to the Christians (present by implication since verse 6b) now comes to explicit statement. The Thessalonians are yet again reminded that they are witnesses to the truth of what Paul claims (cf. again in 2 Th. 3.7).

labour and toil: the two words are coupled again in 2 Th. 3.8 and 2 C. 11.27, the latter, toil, appearing nowhere else in the New Testament. On 'labour', cf. 1.3. 'Toil' refers to the trouble and pain of arduous work. The two words together have a certain assonance.

It was the custom in Pharisaic Judaism for pious Jews to learn a trade: it was felt that to make a living by teaching the law was somehow immoral (cf. the saying 'Make not of the Torah a crown wherewith to aggrandise thyself, nor a spade wherewith to dig' in Pirqe Aboth (*Sayings of the Fathers*) 4.7), and that every Pharisee should be able to maintain himself. Paul's trade is described in Ac. 18.3 as 'tent-maker', but the word used seems to have had the wider sense of any worker in leather (cf. Dibelius, *Paul*, pp. 37, 77). He toiled at his trade not only in Thessalonica but, according to Ac. 18.3, at Corinth too. We have no knowledge as to what work Silvanus and Timothy undertook, and Ac. 20.34 indicates that at times Paul supported his companions. Besides their own contribution, the missionaries were helped whilst at Thessalonica by contributions sent from Philippi (cf. Phil. 4.16).

night and day: the meaning is clearly that Paul was constantly occupied. The order 'night and day' (unlike our 'day and night') is probably due just to Paul's style (it was the common order in Greek and Latin), as also in 3.10 and 2 Th. 3.8 (but contrast e.g. Lk. 18.7). As with us, the expression means both night and day rather than all through the night and all through the day.

preached to you the gospel of God. ¹⁰ You are witnesses, and God
also, how holy and righteous and blameless was our behaviour to
you believers; ¹¹ for you know how, like a father with his children,
we exhorted each one of you and encouraged you and charged you
¹² to lead a life worthy of God, who calls you into his own
kingdom and glory.

---

burden: the Greek word is from the same root as that translated in verse 6,
'made demands', which tends to confirm our interpretation of that verse. Later
(2 Th. 3.7) Paul cites his self-support as an example to others not to burden (the
same word is used) their fellows.

while we preached: this verb, *kērussō*, means to proclaim as a herald, publicly
and solemnly. It occurs in the LXX a number of times, in Zeph. 3.14 and Zech.
9.9, meaning a jubilant shout which welcomes salvation. It is used in the New
Testament regularly of the preaching of the Baptist, of Jesus, and of the disciples.
Paul often uses another word, *euangelizō*, our 'evangelize', and if there is a
distinction to be made it is that *euangelizō* stresses the content while *kērussō*
emphasizes the manner of the proclamation.

10. The climax of Paul's defence of his conduct is now reached. He affirms
solemnly that the missionaries had been in every way beyond reproach.

You are witnesses: 'you' is emphatic, contrasting with those opponents who
suggest what the converts know to be false.

and God also: cf. verse 5.

holy and righteous and blameless: three adverbs are here used which blend
closely together in meaning. They provide the sort of summary of Christian
behaviour such as is found also in Tit. 2.12: possibly Paul did not intend an over-
pedantic distinction to be made between them.

holy: as an adverb this word (*hosiōs*) is found only here in the New Testament,
although the adjective and noun occur more often. In the LXX it is a technical
term for 'the pious ones', but it is not so used in the New Testament. Without
being able to define it more narrowly, its sense here is of conduct religiously and
morally right and good.

righteous: also seldom found, though its adjective occurs some eighty times.
In 1 C. 15.34 it is used as the opposite of 'to sin', whilst in 1 Pet. 2.23 it is used of
God who 'judgeth righteously'. It refers to conformity to a known standard.

blameless: the third adverb is found only here and in 5.23 (where, like the
adjective in 3.13, it means without cause for reproach at Jesus' Parousia).

was our behaviour: Paul is doubtless including in this summary not only his
outward behaviour but also his motives and his intentions (cf. verses 3–6).

believers: the present participle is used, indicating duration. Some commentators
think Paul is opposing the believers to 'unbelievers' or to 'Jews', but doubtless he

would claim to have behaved irreproachably before them too! Most probably
he is simply using an appropriate appellation, like the 'brethren' in 2.2, meaning
'you Christians'. Probably the Jewish smear campaign was suggesting that Paul
had tried to dupe the converts and exploit them.

11. What was involved in proclaiming the gospel is now broken down into
various parts.

like a father: the close relationship between the missionaries and their converts
(cf. 'brethren', in 2.2) and Paul's parental care towards them (2.7–8) is expressed
here in a new image, the very antithesis of an uncaring charlatan (for the same
image cf 1 C. 4.14; 2 C. 6.13; Gal. 4.19).

The Nestle Greek text divides the verses here after 'children', but RSV with RV
and NEB divide after 'charged you'. Wherever we decide to divide, the sense
must be allowed to flow on without break between these two verses.

we exhorted: the first of three present participles by which Paul describes the
mission at Thessalonica. The Greek *parakaleō*, is an intensive word which can mean
'summon', 'call to aid', 'comfort' and 'appeal', and is variously (and frequently)
used in the New Testament. If the primary meaning here is 'urgently appeal'
(urging the converts to apply themselves to their new faith, cf. Ac. 2.40), there is
also the secondary sense of gentle consolation.

each one of you: the expression means what it says, not 'all of you' in a more
general sense. Although the apostles preached at times to large numbers (cf. Ac.
2.41) Paul's normal practice seems to have been to preach to a congregation such
as a synagogue would hold (Ac. 17.1 says that he did this at Thessalonica), and to
concern himself with his converts individually.

encouraged you: a verb used by Paul only here and in 5.14 (the noun he uses
also twice, 1 C. 14.3 and Phil. 3.1). Its meaning is very similar to the word rendered
above ('exhort'), especially since it too can have both the sense of 'encourage' and
'console', although here the idea of consolation is primary (in Jn 11.19, 31—the
only other New Testament occurrences—it means comfort of the bereaved).

charged you: this verb is from the same root meaning 'witness' that we have
already met in verses 5 and 10. In the form used here it can mean both to attest
and to remind.

12. to lead a life: in Greek 'that you should walk'. Paul is specially fond of
this expression by which he signifies man's moral progress through life. In the
LXX the expression has metaphorical and real meaning: classical Greek uses it
generally in the literal sense. The Hebrews were familiar with the metaphor since
their nomad days, when life was literally a journey. Akin to this metaphor is the
description of the Christian faith as 'the way' (Ac. 9.2).

worthy of God: the expression has nothing to do with the 'dignity of the
Christian life' as some scholars suggest, but with its ethical demands. In Col.
1.10 it is explained in terms of 'bearing fruit in every good work' (cf. also
Eph. 4.1; Phil. 1.27). The Christian is to reflect his Lord's own character (cf.
Mt. 5.48).

13 And we also thank God constantly for this, that when you received the word of God which you heard from us, you accepted it not as the word of men but as what it really is, the word of God, which is at work in you believers. 14 For you, brethren, became imitators of the churches of God in Christ Jesus which are in Judea;

---

who calls you: a few (some important) MSS have 'called', as in Gal. 1.6, but the present is here better attested and draws attention to the continuous nature of God's call. (Contrast 4.7, and 1 C. 1.9, where the past tense emphasizes the initial invitation.) The expression comes again in 5.24 bound up, as here, with the expectation of the Parousia of Jesus.

into his own kingdom and glory: the idea of the kingdom of God is prominent in the gospels. Its meaning is influenced by Old Testament usage where it describes God's present kingship and also the awaited manifestation of that kingship in (a) blessing of the just, (b) punishment of the wicked and (c) the renewal of all things. In the Gospels it is intimately associated with the person of Jesus and is thought of as somehow present with him: in his person the awaited declaration of God's sovereignty occurs, and yet in an unexpectedly hidden and mysterious way. It is therefore still awaited in its open, universal, manifest form—particularly in the open manifestation of Christ at his Parousia (for a fuller treatment of this theme in the gospels, see C. E. B. Cranfield, *Mark*, pp. 63–68). Paul seldom uses the expression (eight times), but his thought elsewhere is not essentially different. There is the same strange tension and duality between, on the one hand, the establishment of God's rule by the enactment, in the person of Jesus, of the 'End' events (in him the judgment was enacted, cf. Rom. 6.10; 2 C. 5.14f., etc., the final blessing of the just was accomplished, cf. Rom. 3.24f.; Eph. 1.3, etc., and the subjugation of rebellious powers and renewal of all things happened, cf. Eph. 1.20ff.; Phil. 2.9), and on the other hand, the hope and straining after a still future unambiguous display of this which has happened only in a mystery. Already one can, according to Paul, participate in the 'End' events because of their proleptic occurrence in Christ, but one participates 'by faith', all the time straining towards (cf. Rom. 8.23) the open, unambiguous display of the Kingdom. The tension arising from this backward look and forward hope runs throughout Paul's teaching. In this verse he means two things: (1) that God is calling the converts to present participation in the 'new order', to proleptic entry into the established kingdom of God by commitment to Jesus Christ: and (2) that God is calling the converts to a future participation in the rule of God as it will one day be made universally manifest in the revelation of Jesus Christ in his proper glory (the use of 'glory' here and frequently elsewhere suggests this aspect). In both senses, present proleptic and final unambiguous participation, the thought is parallel to 1.9–10.

THE MANNER IN WHICH THE GOSPEL WAS RECEIVED **2.13–16**

After this protracted defence against apparent charges (or at least the risk of them) of being wandering cheats, Paul dwells for a while on the way the converts responded to the gospel—a theme already broached in 1.6ff.

13. And we also: some think that on account of this emphatic introduction of a new section, Paul is answering a letter from the Thessalonians (cf. also 4.9, 13; 5.1 and the repeated 'you know' which they interpret as 'you said'). But there is no real evidence for this, and Paul would know of the Thessalonians' state from Timothy's report: the construction here can mean simply, 'and we for our part'.

thank God constantly: see 1.2.

you received: *paralambanō* is the verb here which is used by Paul of the transmission of the gospel message and of its ethical and practical consequences (1 C. 11.23, 15.1; Gal. 1.9, 12; 1 Th. 4.1; 2 Th. 3.6; ? Phil. 4.9): it seems to have become almost a technical term in the early church's missionary vocabulary.

the word of God which you heard: lit. 'the heard word from us of God'—a typically Pauline compression of thought combining 'heard word' and 'word of God'.

you accepted: the same verb as in 1.6. The exact difference between this word and *paralambanō* earlier is difficult to define for they are practically synonymous. The RSV rendering 'receive' and 'accept' gets as near to the shift of nuance as possible, the verb here (as suggested under 1.6) having the idea of welcoming.

not as the word of men: the Greek is more definite, 'you received not a word of man'. The idea is the same, but is more forcibly expressed than RSV (and RV and NEB) translates. The gospel proclaimed was no mere human thing and the converts had recognized this (contrast, e.g., the Athenians' interest without recognition of this truth and therefore without 'acceptance', Ac. 17.18ff.).

which is at work: 'which' refers the activity to 'the word', not to 'God' (contrast the Vulgate *qui*). The verb is in a form (middle mood) which can have a passive sense, 'is made effective', but in any case the meaning is that it is ultimately God himself who, through his word, is at work. The verb used generally refers in the New Testament to divine action (cf. 1 C. 2.6, 2.11; Gal. 2.8; Eph. 1.11; 3.20; Phil. 2.13; Col. 1.29) and so comes to mean *effective* action. Elsewhere it is generally used of supernatural power, but not distinctly divine (cf. Mt. 14.2; Mk 6.14) or else demonic (Eph. 2.2; 2 Th. 2.7). It is typical of Paul (and the New Testament as a whole) to link acceptance of the gospel with marked, visible effects in the subsequent life of the believer (as above in 1.5f.). Somehow (the Holy Spirit is prominent in this respect) the vicarious righteousness of Christ to which faith lays claim is appropriated day by day in a real, ethical reformation in the ordinary affairs of life and in a striking readiness to suffer, in imitation of Christ.

in you believers: see verse 10.

14. An immediate, visible effect of the converts' faith and of the working of the word in them is now elaborated: it had been no more than hinted at in 1.6.

for you suffered the same things from your own countrymen as
they did from the Jews, ¹⁵ who killed both the Lord Jesus and the
prophets, and drove us out, and displease God and oppose all men
¹⁶ by hindering us from speaking to the Gentiles that they may be

---

became imitators: see on 1.6.

of the churches of God in Christ Jesus: for 'church', see on 1.1. The plural is
not unnatural here, indicating the various scattered communities of Christians
throughout Judea (cf. 'the churches of Galatia', Gal. 1.2, etc.). 'Church of God'
would, of course, have meant to a Jew 'the Jewish people', but Paul immediately
distinguishes between unbelieving Jews and believing Christians who, recognizing
in Jesus the Messiah of God, are *really* the people of God: so he writes 'churches of
God *in Christ Jesus*'. 'In Christ' is a favourite and decisive expression of Paul's,
signifying (1) God's dealings with the world through the representative Jesus
Christ (cf. e.g. Rom. 3.24f., 'redemption in Christ Jesus') and (2) appropriation of
God's work in Christ by faith, whereby the believer is (so to speak) aligned with
Christ and already shares the benefits of his redemption (cf. e.g. Rom. 6.11; 1 C.
4.10; 2 C. 5.17; Gal. 2.4, etc.). Here 'in Christ' is appropriate both because God's
call was delivered through Christ's work and words and also because the response
to that call was made by affiliation to Christ.

which are in Judea: these communities are cited both because they had suffered
persecution from their inception (cf. Ac. 7.54ff.; 8.1), and also because their trials
had the added, treacherous touch of being perpetrated by their fellow-
countrymen.

you suffered: basically the word used here, *paschein*, means in Greek to be acted
upon rather than to act, and could, according to its qualifying adverb, mean
'well off' or 'suffer ill'. Without any adverb to qualify it, it regularly indicated
misfortune. This is the usage also in the LXX and in the New Testament (although
cf. Gal. 3.3, where the sense seems to be neutral). It is the regular word for Christ's
sufferings, its occurrence in this verse thus emphasizing the unity between his
passion and Christians' trials (further stressed in the next verse).

from your own countrymen: the parallel is not between Jewish Christians in
Judea who suffered from their fellow-Jews, and Gentile Christians in Thessalonica,
who suffered from fellow-Gentiles—in the Judean churches there were doubtless
some Gentile Christians, and in the Thessalonian church doubtless some Jewish
Christians (cf. Ac. 17.4). Further, it was the jealous *Jews* who, according to Ac.
17.5, incited trouble at Thessalonica. The parallel is that in both cases the troublemakers were kith and kin, fellow-countrymen and fellow-citizens. *Sumphuletēs*,
translated 'countryman', occurs only here in the New Testament and means in
Greek both 'of the same race' and 'of the same stock'.

from the Jews: Paul often enough speaks of 'the Jews' in distinction from 'the

Gentiles' (e.g. Rom. 1.16; 2.9; 10.12; 1 C. 1.22; Gal. 3.28; Col. 3.11, etc.) and here he makes no special pejorative stress. We may contrast the usage in the fourth gospel, where the writer regularly means by 'the Jews' the opponents of Christ (cf. Jn 2.18, 20; 6.41; 7.1, etc.).

15. The treachery of jealous Jews touches off Paul's indignant account of their crimes.

who killed both the Lord Jesus: the construction with 'both . . . and', suggesting correlatives, cannot be taken to mean that for Paul Christ's death and the death of the prophets were of equal weight, wickedness, or value, for his constant stress on Christ's death and its redemptive significance excludes such an idea. Rather it emphasizes the essential unity between the martyrdom of God's messengers, the prophets, and Christ's crucifixion (as in the parable, Mk 12.1–12). Unbelieving Jews of all times are taken here as essentially one (cf. also in Mt. 23.29ff.; Ac. 7.51f.). The unspeakable wickedness of the crime committed by the Jews is underlined by 'the Lord': the Jews had actually killed God.

and the prophets: Israel's guilt in this respect is known already in the Old Testament (cf. 1 Kg. 19.10; Neh. 9.26; Jer. 2.30). We cannot tell if Paul was thinking specially of the contemporary slaying of the Baptist, but he might have been.

and drove us out: the dreadful wickedness of the Jews in crucifying Christ did not begin there, nor, as Paul now declares, did it stop at that. The verb used here is a compound found nowhere else in the New Testament. In its simple form (*diōkō*) it means to pursue, thence in the sense of 'hunting down' it comes to mean 'to persecute', which is its usual meaning in the New Testament (cf. Lk. 21.12; Jn 5.16; Rom. 12.14). With the prefix *ek*, 'out', as here, it probably means 'drove out with the intention of persecuting'. (If Paul had in mind especially what happened at Thessalonica, it would be true to say that the missionaries had in point of fact beaten a hasty retreat: yet, noting the cause of their departure, it is fair to say that this retreat amounted to being chased out.) 'Us' probably means more specifically than 'we Christians' the apostles of Christ (cf. 2.6). In Eph. 2.20 Paul couples apostles and prophets beside Jesus Christ, and in 1 C. 4.9 gives to apostles a prominent place in suffering. Here he probably means that just as the emissaries of God in the old covenant were persecuted, so also the special agents of Christ in the new order are rejected by the Jews.

and displease God: the indictment, besides listing the persecution of Jesus and his spokesmen before and after him, goes on to two more general statements: this is the first. The present participle indicates a lasting state. On the meaning of 'please', see 2.4.

and oppose all men: this is the second general statement. 'All men', as we see from 2 C. 3.2; Phil. 4.5, etc., means 'men at large'. Paul means more than the sullen inhumanity of the Jews to which various classical authors refer, as the next verse indicates.

16. **hindering us:** the way in which the Jews oppose men generally is in their

saved—so as always to fill up the measure of their sins. But God's wrath has come upon them at last!

17 But since we were bereft of you, brethren, for a short time, in

---

antagonism to the Christian mission, not simply because they caused difficulties and contention (sometimes jealousy and quarrelsomeness could, in a way, further the gospel's progress: cf. Phil. 1.15ff.), but because through their hostility the missionaries were forced to move on from place to place before their work was properly completed.

from speaking: see on 1.8.

to the Gentiles: Paul's particular mission was, he believed, to evangelize the Gentiles (cf. Ac. 9.15; 13.26, 47; 15.7; Rom. 1.13; 15.16; Eph. 3.1). The word 'Gentile' (*ethnē*) means basically 'nation' or 'people'. In the New Testament it is sometimes used of the Jewish nation (e.g. Lk. 7.5; Ac. 10.22). Generally, however, it means people and nations other than Jewish (where *ethnē* corresponds to the Old Testament's general distinction between 'the heathen' and the 'chosen people': we may compare the secular use of the time of 'barbarian', which distinguished those who knew Greek and Greek manners from those who did not). 'Gentile' can, however, also be used in opposition to 'Christian' (as in 1 C. 5.1, 12.2; 1 Th. 4.5) perhaps because Christians belong to the 'new Israel' (cf. Rom. 2.28ff.; Gal. 6.16), and in Eph. 3.1 (? Rom. 11.13 too) Paul even speaks of Gentile Christians as Gentiles.

that they may be saved: to understand what Paul means by salvation we must turn back to the Old Testament, where we find a longing for God to intervene in history favourably for Israel, avenging his chosen people and overcoming everything contrary to his will. The belief grew up that nothing short of a total intervention on a cosmic dimension would suffice for this.

The fundamental belief of the New Testament writers is that this intervention took place in Jesus Christ. The tension referred to under verse 12 (above) applies very much here too. As the decisive events lie in the past, Paul can speak of salvation both as a present possibility and reality (cf. 1 C. 1.18; 2 C. 2.15; Eph. 2.5; etc.) to be appropriated by faith, and also, since the decisive events occurred in a hidden manner demanding clarification, as a future hope, an event which will one day be revealed (cf. Rom. 5.10; 13.11; 1 Th. 5.8; 1 Pet. 1.5). As Rom. 1.16 makes clear, salvation is deliverance from God's wrath (though occasionally in the New Testament it refers to rescue of a mundane sort; cf. Ac. 27.20, 31).

to fill up the measure of their sins: 'to' is ambiguous in Greek, and might indicate purpose (in order to) or consequence (with the result that). It is very common in Paul, and if here he meant 'in order that' then clearly it could only be in the sense of a *divine* purpose (similar to 2 Th. 2.11; cf. Rom. 1.24). But most scholars agree that the emphasis here is upon consequence: the effect of the Jews' opposition is to add sin upon sin (cf. NEB, 'they have been making up the full measure of their guilt'). The words reflect Gen. 15.16, but the sense is probably akin to rabbinic thought in which man's life is 'measured out' to him according to a divine plan. The word rendered 'sin' is *hamartia*, a common word in the New Testament and one whose meaning Paul defines in Rom. 3.23 as 'falling short of the glory of God', i.e. not attaining to the perfection of God and the perfection intended by God for man. In Paul's thought, sin is an external power to which man becomes enslaved (cf. Rom. 6.17) and which 'pays' its servants with death (Rom. 6.23). Less frequently, Paul uses other words to express various aspects of sin: *anomia*, lit. contrary to what is lawful, *adikia*, lit. contrary to what is just, and *parabasis*, lit. going aside (from the right way).

God's wrath: see on 1.10. The best MSS have simply 'the wrath', but the addition in others of 'God's' makes explicit the sense intended.

is come: the Greek is in the aorist tense, which often indicates past time. The same word as used here comes in Mt.12.28 (par. Lk. 11.20) concerning the Kingdom of God, and scholars have long discussed its precise meaning: it has two possible senses in Greek; 'to anticipate' and 'to arrive'. It is rarely used in the New Testament. In 1 Th. 4.15 it certainly means 'to anticipate' (in the sense of precede), but in e.g. Rom. 9.31 it means 'to arrive'. The ambiguity, we suggest, is particularly apt, and is perhaps intentional in this verse in view of the tension referred to (above, and see on 1.10) concerning the wrath of God proleptically revealed already (in the death of Christ) and yet still to be finally and openly revealed (in the events accompanying Christ's Parousia). There is no support for the view advocated by a few scholars (mainly of the Tübingen school) that this is an historical reference to the fall of Jerusalem in A.D. 70.

at last: this could be understood (with AV and RV) qualitatively as 'to the uttermost', or 'fully'. It could, on the other hand, be understood temporally as 'finally' (cf. NEB, 'for good and all'). The same problem arises in interpreting Mk 13.13 and Jn 13.1. It is probable that here the meaning of the whole expression will be that God's wrath has been declared in Jesus Christ in its final 'End' character (and so also, secondarily, 'to the uttermost').

PAUL'S CONCERN FOR THE THESSALONIAN CHRISTIANS
2.17–3.13

PAUL'S DESIRE TO REVISIT THE THESSALONIANS 2.17–20

The apostles' forced departure from Thessalonica before the completion of their work was a source of great sorrow to them. This part of the letter follows quite naturally from the first section: after the mission itself, already discussed, came the longing to return and the stop-gap mission of Timothy, who was to report on the converts' state and to bring to them some further help and teaching.

17. But we: seems to contrast with the 'for you brethren' in verse 4. It is certainly emphatic, 'as for us . . .'.

person not in heart, we endeavoured the more eagerly and with
great desire to see you face to face; ¹⁸ because we wanted to come
to you—I, Paul, again and again—but Satan hindered us. ¹⁹ For

---

bereft of you: the Greek word (found only here in the New Testament) is very
expressive, meaning literally 'being made orphans'. The word could be used of a
parentless child, or of childless parents, and even in a general sense of any severe
deprivation or desolation. Its use here continues the thought of verses 7 and 11
that Paul had been deprived of his beloved children. 'Of you' is so expressed in
Greek (*aph' humōn*, in place of a simple genitive) as to emphasize the enforced
nature of the deprivation. The whole could be rendered, 'having been torn away
from you'.

for a short time: the construction of the Greek is unique, using two words
expressing a short or limited period. The second word (*hōra*) is found frequently
in the gospels but seldom in Paul, and it generally (though with some important
exceptions) means a particular moment in time. The first word (*kairos*) is used
often by Paul, and means (almost without exception) a season or duration of time,
particularly with reference to its propitious character, its special purpose or its
significant content (cf. e.g. Rom. 13.11, 'knowing the time . . .'; 2 C. 6.2, 'I have
heard thee in a time accepted . . .'). The New Testament knows yet another word
for time, *chronos*, which generally denotes time in its chronological aspect (see
on 5.1).

in person not in heart: the Thessalonians must not imagine that enforced
separation can make Paul forget them. 'In person' renders the Greek word for
'face' (the same word occurs again later in this verse, rendered in RSV 'face to
face', in RV 'face'). But from this straightforward meaning it came to embrace
the idea of the external form or appearance of someone, and so came to mean 'a
person'. On 'heart' see 2.4.

we endeavoured the more eagerly: the Greek *spoudazō* means much more than
our 'try', combining the ideas of haste and earnestness. Paul uses the same word
again in Gal. 2.10 and Eph. 4.3 (where RSV renders 'eagerly'). Here 'endeavoured
eagerly' captures the sense.

the more: is the comparative form of the adverb exceedingly. It is not certain if
Paul intended a strict comparative force, however, since this form sometimes in
common Greek takes over the meaning of the superlative, 'most exceedingly'.
Sometimes in the New Testament the comparative sense is certainly intended
(cf. e.g. 2 C. 11.23; Gal. 1.14; Phil. 1.14) and at other times the exact meaning is
uncertain (as here, and cf. 2 C. 1.12; 7.5). If we take the comparative form
seriously, we need, in order to complete the sense, to understand 'more
exceedingly because of our affection for you', or 'more exceedingly because we
were prevented', or 'because of your situation' (cf. 3.3). Since such a completion

of sense is not made explicit it is probable that Paul intended the superlative.

and with great desire: this word in the New Testament almost always has a bad sense ('lust', 'evil desire'), although Lk. 22.15 and Phil. 1.23 are instances where, as here, it denotes good intention.

face to face: lit. 'to see your face', i.e. to see you.

18. The efforts to revisit them, spoken of in verse 17, are grounded in the simple desire expressed here (besides the desire to complete the work already started in Thessalonica; 3.2f., 10).

we wanted: it is a matter of debate between scholars how this verb, *thelō*, relates to the other frequent New Testament word for 'wish', *boulomai*, and whether its sense is stronger or weaker: (cf. RSV 'wanted' with NEB 'we did propose'). It seems likely, since Paul expressed himself so strongly in verse 17, that 'wanted' here, understood as a real desire, reflects the meaning he intended.

I, Paul: this is the first of a number of instances where Paul speaks for himself alone in these letters (cf. also 3.5, 5.27; 2 Th. 2.5; 3.17). Clearly, Paul was the leader of the group of missionaries and probably also the special object of the Jews' jealous hatred. It is not unnatural that he most especially wanted to get back to Thessalonica and further the work already begun.

again and again: RSV paraphrases a difficult expression, lit. 'and once and twice'. The phrase 'once and twice' is found in the LXX four times, always meaning 'repeatedly'. In the New Testament it occurs here and in Phil. 4.16 (where its precise meaning is also debatable). The expression is complicated by the first 'and', which could give the sense 'both once and twice' (and some commentators incline to accept this, with RV 'once and again'). But possibly the first 'and' serves to introduce the entire idea and the words 'once and twice' have a more general application meaning 'oftentimes' rather than the definite 'on two occasions'. This seems to give better sense to Paul's 'when we could bear it no longer' (3.1) than would merely two foiled attempts.

Satan: the word comes from Hebrew, and means basically 'an accuser' or 'adversary', but in the history of Israel it came to mean the supernatural and supreme adversary of man (cf. Job 1.6; Zech. 3.1) and so became a proper name for the devil. Paul does not use it very frequently (some eight times) having many other terms by which to describe the forces ranged against man and against God (e.g. 'the evil one', 2 Th. 3.3; 'the god of this world', 2 C. 4.4; 'the tempter', 1 Th. 3.5; 'the devil', Eph. 4.27). 'Satan' here introduces us to Paul's dualism which, if inherited from his Pharisaic upbringing, was decisively conditioned by his acceptance of Christianity. For Paul, this world (or 'age' as he says) is dominated by evil (cf. 1 C. 2.6; Eph. 6.12, etc.). Like his Jewish kin, therefore, he strains for the inbreak of God's rule to overthrow these evil powers (2 Th. 1.8f.). But the situation is not simple: the opposition is not merely between the coming (good) age and the present (bad) one, for already the coming age in a sense *has come*, in Jesus Christ, already the 'powers' of this world have been toppled from their exalted height (cf. especially Col. 2.15). The tension spoken of earlier (cf. verse 12) is still

what is our hope or joy or crown of boasting before our Lord Jesus at his coming? Is it not you? ²⁰ For you are our glory and joy.

3 Therefore when we could bear it no longer, we were willing to be left behind at Athens alone, ² and we sent Timothy, our

---

to the fore because the 'powers' retain a certain force and are still at work (Eph. 6.12), the presence of the new age is discernible only by faith (the evil forces themselves certainly did not realize what, in Jesus Christ, was actually happening; cf. 1 C. 2.8), and the longing for the final, unambiguous display of God's rule is more intense than ever.

hindered: in later Greek this word was used in a military sense of making a break through the enemies' lines. There is no clue here about the way in which Satan thwarted Paul's wishes. Various suggestions have been made: some think of sickness, others of a surety demanded of the converts by the civic authorities at Thessalonica that the missionaries would not return. But evidence for a firm decision either way is lacking, and it may be that Paul intended us to understand 'difficulties in general'. Paul sometimes discerns a divine purpose behind obstacles (Ac. 16.6f.), but not in this case.

19. The thought of the Parousia of Christ is never far from Paul's mind and probably the mention of Satan brings to explicit statement the picture of the missionaries and their converts at Christ's return, the time when Satan will be completely put down (2 Th. 2.3ff.). Besides, the desire to go back to Thessalonica was in order to establish the converts in their faith with a view to their being made ready for the Parousia (3.10, 13).

For what is: an exclamation which might also mean, 'for who is?'

our hope: the thought is probably that the Thessalonians, amongst others, are to prove that Paul has faithfully exercised his ministry (cf. Phil. 2.16), though it could be that the converts, through faithfulness, will be 'unblamable in holiness' (3.13) at the Parousia.

our joy: see on 1.6.

or crown of boasting: Greek has two words for crown, the one being a sign of royalty (*diadēma*) and the other (the one used regularly in the New Testament apart from *diadēma* three times in Revelation), *stephanos*, meaning, as here, a garland expressing honour or victory or festal rejoicing. Paul regards it as a picture of the Christian's final reward (cf. 1 C. 9.25). Here the Thessalonians are regarded as Paul's emblem of work well done and of victory achieved (cf. also Phil. 4.1).

boasting: a word which, with its counterparts, is found in the New Testament almost solely in Paul. It denotes not only an inward gladness but the outward expression of this (RV translates it by 'glorying'). It is forbidden where the object concerned is unworthy (cf. 1 C. 1.29 'flesh'; 3.21 'in men'; 2 C. 5.12 'in appearance') or where its object makes glorying unfitting (Rom. 3.27). In 2 C. 11–12 it is used in the sense of 'to brag', but generally Paul uses it of a legitimate expression of good achievement.

before our Lord Jesus: 'Before', as in 1.3, means 'in the presence of'. On the title 'Lord Jesus' see on 1.1.

at his coming: the Greek word *Parousia* simply means presence, and is used in the New Testament sometimes of an ordinary human arrival or presence (1 C. 16.17; 2 C. 7.6f., 10.10; Phil. 1.26, 2.12). There is evidence in papyri and certain inscriptions that the word came to be used of a royal visit. In the Christian vocabulary it quickly became a technical term for the return of Christ in his glory at the end of time (and is already in process of becoming such a technical term in this sense in the New Testament). The New Testament also uses other words of this return of Christ: *epiphaneia*, appearing, in e.g. 1 Tim. 6.14; *apokalupsis*, revelation, in e.g. 2 Th. 1.7; and it can speak of it simply as 'day', as in 2 Th. 2.2; 2 Tim. 1.18.

Is it not you: the position of this clause in the Greek is between 'crown of boasting' and 'before our Lord Jesus Christ'. Grammatically it could, therefore, be taken with what follows, as in RV 'are not ye before our Lord . . .'. Probably however, the remark is intended as a parenthesis and RSV wisely changes the word-order to give this sense. The Greek reads 'is it not you also', 'also' being lit. 'and', which might be meant in a general sense 'and is it not you?', but which perhaps is meant in the sense of 'as well', indicating the Thessalonians in company with the other churches founded by Paul.

20. For: in such a construction means 'indeed' (cf. NEB).

you are: the present tense is used, for the Thessalonians are already that which at the Parousia they will be *seen* to be.

glory: the honour suggested by 'crown of boasting' in verse 19.

TIMOTHY'S VISIT TO THESSALONICA AND HIS REPORT 3.1–10

1. Therefore: the chapter-division means nothing here, the sense following directly on from the desire expressed in 2.17ff.

we could bear it: the verb used here is found in the New Testament only in this verse and in verse 5, and in 1 C. 9.12, 13.7. In Greek it meant originally 'to cover something' with a view to protecting it: so it came to mean both to ward off or repel, and also to conceal or hide. Later, the former meaning developed further to signify 'to endure', and this is probably the sense Paul intended here (as in its other occurrences seems also the case).

we were willing: see on 2.8.

to be left behind: strangely, this verb is used elsewhere by Paul only in Old Testament citations (Rom. 11.4 from 1 Kg. 19.18, and Eph. 5.31 from Gen. 2.24). It has the sense of abandoning someone or something and can be used of departure in death (Mk 12.19). 'Willing to be forsaken' would give the nuance here.

at Athens: a free city, even under the Romans, though belonging to the Province

brother and God's servant in the gospel of Christ, to establish you in your faith and to exhort you, ³ that no one be moved by these afflictions. You yourselves know that this is to be our lot. ⁴ For when we were with you, we told you beforehand that we were to suffer

---

of Achaia. Even in New Testament times it still held a fascination for anyone interested in culture and philosophy, and was a university city to which students from all over the known world came. Luke's description of the inhabitants (Ac. 17.16–22) is supported by information from secular sources. According to Ac. 17, Paul, Silas and Timothy moved from Thessalonica to Beroea first, evangelizing there until the Jews who created trouble before came on and caused faction at Beroea too. Paul then went directly to Athens, leaving instructions that Silas and Timothy should follow him directly (Ac. 17.15).

alone: in Greek this word is in the plural, which might be simply a matter of style, continuing the plural throughout the letter, but in fact meaning here Paul only: or it might mean Paul and Silas. We just do not know exactly when Timothy and Silas rejoined Paul. Ac. 18.5 gives the impression that it was only after Paul had left Athens and was settled in Corinth, but it appears from this letter that Timothy arrived certainly whilst Paul was still at Athens and was sent off on his mission to Thessalonica. Perhaps he arrived with Silas and after his departure Paul and Silas were left 'alone'; or perhaps Paul sent Silas also off on a mission (see Introduction p. 4); or possibly Silas only arrived later when Paul had already reached Corinth, having stayed longer than Timothy in Beroea. We cannot be certain.

2. our brother: unlike 'brethren' (1.4, 2.1, etc.), Paul means more than 'fellow-Christian'. He means that Timothy is a colleague.

God's servant: The word in Greek, *sunergos*, really means 'fellow-worker' (cf. Rom. 16.21, 'Timothy my fellow-worker' where the same word is used). But we cannot be certain that Paul wrote this, for some good MSS read 'minister (*diakonos*) of God'. (Some other MSS read 'minister of God and our fellow-servant' and others 'and servant' but probably these arose from one or other of the two better attested readings.) Paul can and does speak of his fellow-workers as 'ministers' of Christ or of God (Col. 1.7; Eph. 6.21), but possibly 'fellow-worker' is here the original reading, for (1) 'fellow-worker of God' is a startling expression, likely to be altered to—though hardly from—'minister'; (2) 1 C. 3.9 shows that Paul could speak in this way; (3) if, as we suggest, 'brother' here means 'colleague' then 'fellow-worker (or colleague) of God' makes a suitable parallel.

gospel of Christ: see on 1.5.

to establish you: the metaphorical sense of a verb meaning basically 'to set fast' or 'fix' (as in Lk. 16.26). Paul uses the verb six times, four times of God establishing

Christians. It signifies keeping loyal to the faith and living increasingly in a manner appropriate to and demanded by this faith. It is probable, as some scholars suggest, that this word belonged to the early church's technical vocabulary.

in your faith: the preposition (*huper*) is variously used by Paul, sometimes meaning 'for the sake of' or 'on behalf of' (e.g. 1 Th. 5.10), and sometimes meaning 'concerning' (e.g. 2 Th. 1.4). RSV 'in' nicely retains the two possibilities. The phrase in the Greek could be taken with both verbs (i.e. 'to establish you and exhort (you) in your faith') or with the second verb only (i.e. 'to establish you, and to exhort you in your faith'), but it is difficult to take it (as RSV does) with the first only (NEB at this point is quite a paraphrase).

to exhort you: the same verb as in 2.11. The same expression (in reverse order) comes in 2 Th. 2.17 of an activity of God. We find within the same two letters Paul's view that human faith is both an action of God and human activity (cf. Phil. 2.12f. for the two ideas immediately juxtaposed).

3. Paul's constant fear was that his converts would, either by persuasive opponents of the faith or by adverse circumstances, abandon their new allegiance. His anxiety here would be the greater in view of his hasty and premature departure.

that no one be moved: the object of Timothy's mission. The verb, *sainesthai*, is found only here in the New Testament, and scholars are divided as to its meaning here. Properly it means the wagging of a dog's tail, and (presumably because dogs do this generally to ingratiate themselves!) it comes to mean 'to fawn upon' and so 'to beguile' and 'to deceive'. There is a little evidence that it could mean 'to disturb'. Several textual emendations have been proposed because of the difficulty presented by this verb. Clearly the desire to establish and exhort the converts indicates what Paul was afraid might happen: possibly he feared that his converts would be deceived on account of the afflictions, not having understood that to suffer is the Christian's lot. This would give a possible and suitable sense in the context, the verb meaning both 'deceive' and 'disturb'.

by these afflictions: 'by' might be temporal ('moved in the course of these afflictions') but gives here better sense as the instrument. For 'affliction', see on 1.6. There is no need to decide whether Paul meant his own troubles at Corinth or those afflicting the converts, for it seems probable that both would have been in Paul's mind at the time of writing.

this is to be our lot: the verb *keimai*, is a present indicative, but is practically the equivalent of a perfect. RV 'hereunto we are appointed', is more literal than RSV, and gives the sense to the verb that was probably intended: it has already been determined that such is to be the nature of the Christian life. The theme of suffering as the lot of the Christian is by no means confined to Paul: cf. e.g. Mk 13.9–13; Jn 15.20ff.; Ac. 14.22; 1 Pet. 4.12–19.

4. For when we were with you: an expression reproduced exactly, though with a slight variation of order, in 2 Th. 3.10.

we told you beforehand: the tense here is imperfect, denoting a continuous

affliction; just as it has come to pass, and as you know. [5] For this reason, when I could bear it no longer, I sent that I might know your faith, for fear that somehow the tempter had tempted you and that our labour would be in vain.

6 But now that Timothy has come to us from you, and has brought us the good news of your faith and love and reported that

---

action or one often repeated. 'We repeatedly told you' is the meaning.

we were to suffer affliction: lit. 'we are about to be afflicted' (Greek *mellomen thlibesthai*). Paul seldom uses a verb in the present tense following *mellein* ('to be about to') (cf. Rom. 4.24 and 8.13), but where he does, the certainty of fulfilment is uppermost. Add to this fact the general usage of *mellō* in the New Testament, which is to stress the strong probability or real certainty of something, and we see how much weight Paul laid on the inevitability of suffering for the Christians. See further on 2 Th. 2.

just as it has come to pass and as you know: great emphasis is placed here and in verse 3 on the converts' knowledge of the facts and of the apostles' teaching. We hear no more of this until 4.1 and after.

5. For this reason: the thoughts expressed in verses 2–4 are now summed up and the theme of verse 2 is reiterated.

when I could bear it no longer: the 'I' is emphatic (cf. 'we' similarly in 2.17). If Paul was alone all the time in Athens (see on 3.1 above) and the 'we' in this section is not accurate but simply continues the plural style of the letter, then the first person here will be a reflection of the real situation. If, on the other hand, Timothy (and/or Silas) were with him, the question arises whether some special contrast is intended here by 'when *I* could bear it no longer' between Paul's anxiety and possibly their optimism. The simplest explanation is to link the idea here with 2.17 and to suppose that Paul, the instigator and leader of the mission in Thessalonica, was particularly anxious to see the work completed and that he, above all others, found the enforced separation unbearable. Timothy's mission was, therefore, Paul's idea (and there are no grounds for supposing, as some do, that Paul sent privately a second messenger to see how the converts fared!).

to know: in Greek not the same word as 'you know' (*oida*) in verse 5, etc., but the verb *ginōskō*, which carries a flavour of uncertainty, meaning 'to determine', 'to get to know'.

your faith: '*Pistis*', the Greek word for faith, means first of all allegiance to the gospel proclaimed (as, for example, in verse 2). But the idea of perseverance and of accompanying moral reform is seldom absent: certainly here Paul means something quite general, such as 'your standing in the Christian life'.

for fear that: the Greek *mē*, in such a context, is usually rendered in RV 'lest' (e.g. in 1 C. 8.9; Gal. 2.2) and RSV gives the same sense of apprehension: NEB 'fearing' is, on the other hand, too definite.

the tempter: as a name for the devil, only here and in Mt. 4.3, though 'tempting' (the verb) is described as a function of the devil in Mk 1.13 par., 1 C. 7.5 (and cf. the parallelism in Mt. 6.9 between 'lead us not into temptation' and 'but deliver us from the evil [one]').

had tempted you: the verb has two meanings: 'to prove', 'put to the test', or 'to seek to seduce'. In the New Testament it is used in both senses, in the former in Heb. 3.9 (referring to the Israelites 'putting God to the test' in the wilderness, cf. Exod. 17.7) and 1 C. 10.9 (referring to Num. 21.5ff.): and, more usually, in the latter sense in e.g. Mk 8.11; Gal. 6.1—often describing a human activity (e.g. Mt. 16.1), but sometimes the activity of the devil (cf. above). It is in the sense of 'seducing' that the writer of the Epistle of James affirms that *God* tempts no-one Jas 1.13): Paul, in 1 C. 10.13, allows that God supplies 'ways of escape' so that no-one is tempted beyond endurance. In our verse, the fear is that the converts will have been drawn away from their faith on account of their afflictions, not realizing (as they ought to have, verse 3) that such suffering formed an inevitable corollary of faith.

our labour: as in 1.3, hard, wearying toil.

would be in vain: see on 2.1. The verb here is in the subjunctive mood, expressing more remoteness and improbability than the indicative, used above in 'tempting'. Paul is unwilling to envisage as a strong possibility his work being brought to nothing.

6. But now: a new section begins with an account of Timothy's return and the good news of the converts' faith which he brought. 'Now', in the Greek, is a word (*arti*) that sometimes means the present in general (cf. e.g. Gal. 1.10) and sometimes the present contrasted with the future (cf. e.g. 1 C. 13.12). But it can also refer to the immediate past, 'just now', and this is probably the sense it is supposed to carry here. The letter is being written very soon after Timothy had arrived back.

to us from you: some scholars remark on the frequency of the pronouns 'you' and 'we' in this verse, but we find only what we should expect, considering the subject matter, i.e. an account of Timothy's return and report.

has brought us the good news: lit. 'having evangelized us', the same word being used in the Greek as is elsewhere in the New Testament only used of preaching the gospel (see on 1.5). This indicates how deeply Paul was moved by the allaying of his fears (3.5) and the assurance of the converts' progress in the faith: this was 'gospel' indeed!

your faith: as in verse 5, their situation in relation to the whole Christian life.

and love: on *agapē*, see 1.3. Here the question is, does Paul mean their love towards God or their love for one another (cf. verse 12, which could support the latter or suggest that the latter was lacking!). Once again, the ambiguity might be intentional. For 'faith and love' coupled together, see on 1.3.

T.C.B.: T.—3

you always remember us kindly and long to see us, as we long to see you—⁷ for this reason, brethren, in all our distress and affliction we have been comforted about you through your faith; ⁸ for now we live, if you stand fast in the Lord. ⁹ For what thanksgiving can we render to God for you, for all the joy which we feel for your

---

and reported: the Greek has 'and that': it is convenient in English to supply another verb. But notice that what follows is still part of the 'good news' brought back by Timothy.

you always remember us: Paul uses the same word as in 1.2 translated 'mention', where it referred (as often) to mentioning in prayer (cf. Rom. 1.9; Eph. 1.16; Phil. 1.3; 2 Tim. 1.3; Phm. 4). But the construction with 'kindly' seems to exclude that sense here, and to mean that the converts have pleasant memories of the apostles.

kindly: RSV rendering of *agathēn*. The same word comes again in 5.5 with real ethical import, but in this verse it simply means 'pleasant'.

long: Paul uses here a verb (found elsewhere in the New Testament only eight times) which generally signifies earnest desire (cf. e.g. 2 C. 5.2, 9.14; Phil. 1.8, 2.26).

as we long to see you: lit. 'as we also you'. The affection felt by the missionaries for the converts has already been expressed in 2.7-8, 11, 17-18: Paul now learns, to his comfort, that the desire for a reunion was mutual.

7. The result of Timothy's report is twofold. First, Paul rejoices, gives thanks and prays. Secondly, he gives advice and encouragement in those matters where Timothy has (presumably) indicated that special help or exhortation was needed.

for this reason: there is an anacoluthon here, Paul opening a new section without grammatically completing the previous one: but the meaning is plain enough.

brethren: a specially appropriate term after the mutual longing spoken of in verse 6.

in all our distress and affliction: here (contrast 3.3) it is apparent that Paul means his own difficult situation since leaving Thessalonica (Ac. 18 shows that the Jewish problem experienced there continued at Beroea and Corinth: see further, Intro. pp. 3-4). The word translated 'distress' meant originally 'force' or 'constraint', and came to be used of actual violence or punishment (besides having also a philosophical usage). Paul sometimes uses it meaning constraint (cf. 1 C. 9.16; 2 C. 9.7; Phm. 14), but also uses it in connection with persecution where 'distress' is clearly meant (cf. 2 C. 6.4, 12.10). In conjunction with 'afflictions' this must be the meaning here too. Lk. 21.23 uses the same word of the 'End' woes expected before the final inbreak of the Parousia, and it is possible that Paul intended such an overtone here, inasmuch as the distress could be seen as part of the 'End' disturbances. Such an eschatological overtone would be akin to that contained in the word *thlipsis*, 'affliction', for which see on 1.6. 'All' probably has a general sense meaning 'all manner of. . . .' (contrast in verse 9 below).

we have been comforted: see on 2.11, though here the primary sense is 'consoled'.

through your faith: the converts' faith is the source of Paul's relief. As throughout this section, 'faith' means both commitment and perseverance, so that 'faith' here is the equivalent of 'standing fast in the Lord', cf. verse 8.

8. for now: Paul can use *nun* ('now') as a conjunction meaning 'but' or 'and' (e.g. 2 C. 7.9). The overwhelming majority of times, however, he uses it in a temporal adverbial sense, 'at this time' (sometimes to distinguish between the situation before Christ's coming and that since). Here he refers to the new mood brought about by Timothy's report.

we live: this is present tense indicating a continuing state. Commentators have interpreted the expression variously. Some link it with the thought behind Phil. 1.21ff., the progress of the gospel is the very life of the apostle. Some understand it as eternal life and link it with the thought of 2.19. Others—and this seems most in accord with the sense of the whole passage—refer it to the new 'lease of life' which Timothy's good news had brought Paul (and this accords best with Paul's feelings expressed elsewhere, esp. 1 C. 15.31; 2 C. 14.31ff. 4.7ff.). Weighed down by his burdens in Corinth, he was nonetheless refreshed and given new heart by his converts' satisfactory state.

if you stand fast in the Lord: 'you' is emphatic in the Greek. It may be, as some suggest, that Paul was particularly anxious about the outcome of the Thessalonian mission and that it was a kind of test case. More probably Paul is simply drawing out the comparison between his own situation and theirs: 'we are afflicted: nevertheless, we live if all goes well with *you*'. The verb here is in the indicative (after *ean*, 'if', it is more usually in the subjunctive) which gives to the condition spoken of something of the idea of fulfilment. The verb is a late Greek form which occurs only eight times in the New Testament, seven times in Paul, always with the sense of standing firm (the same verb comes again in 2 Th. 2.15). In Phil. 4.1 Paul writes the same thought as an injunction, 'stand fast in the Lord', (cf. 1 C. 16.13). So the whole verse means, 'if, as we believe you are doing, you continue steadfast in your Christian faith and life, we are revitalized.'

9. Paul's joy now turns into a rhetorical question—then into a prayer.

thanksgiving: *Eucharistia* is from the same root as *charis* (see on 1.1) and is always used by Paul of gratitude to God for some gift of grace. It is the word from which we derive our 'eucharist', though it does not appear in this technical liturgical sense before Ignatius (*c.* A.D. 115) (even 1 C. 14.16 can hardly refer to eucharist in this sense). As Paul knew that his preaching was effective only through God's accompanying power (see 1.5), so he regards his converts' faith not as a personal triumph but as a gift of God's goodness.

render: RV 'render again' and NEB 'return' are more exact. The verb has the sense of reciprocation and is used of repaying with judgment in 2 Th. 1.6 (cf. Rom. 12.19) or, as in 5.15, in a good sense. It frequently carries the idea of paying back

sake before our God, ¹⁰ praying earnestly night and day that we
may see you face to face and supply what is lacking in your faith?
¹¹ Now may our God and Father himself, and our Lord Jesus,
direct our way to you; ¹² and may the Lord make you increase and
abound in love to one another and to all men, as we do to you, ¹³ so
that he may establish your hearts unblamable in holiness before our
God and Father, at the coming of our Lord Jesus with all his saints.

---

what is fitting (as in 2 Th. 1.6; cf. Rom. 2.6, 13.7). So here we might paraphrase,
'what thanksgiving can we fittingly return to God . . .'.
all the joy: 'all' is intensive here, meaning 'so much'
for your sake: i e. 'on account of you', or, 'by reason of you'.
  10. The rhetorical question begun in verse 9 continues by referring to Paul's
constant prayer, and so introduces the actual prayer which comes in verses 11-13.
praying: see on 1.2.
earnestly: as though no word is strong enough to contain his thought, Paul
here uses a double compound meaning 'super-abundantly'—an expression found
in the New Testament only here, in 5.13 and in Eph. 3.20.
night and day: see on 2.9. The sense is as in 1.2 'constantly'.
to see you face to face: on the construction, see 2.17. This gives the contents of
Paul's prayer. His desire to be reunited with his converts is not diminished because
of Timothy's visit and subsequent good report, but is rather intensified.
and supply what is lacking in your faith: a purpose within a purpose. Paul's
desire to return is not simply so as to be with his converts again, but in order to
serve them. The word translated 'supply', *katartizō*, means 'to repair' or 'to fit
out' and so 'to render perfect'. It is used, e.g., in Mk 1.19 of mending fishing nets
damaged in use. Its usual meaning in the New Testament is 'to make fully perfect'
(cf. Gal. 6.1; 1 Pet. 5.10, etc.). RSV 'that which is lacking' translates a noun
(*husterēma*) found only in Paul in the New Testament, apart from Lk. 21.4, where,
as in some half of the occurrences in Paul (2 C. 8.14 (twice), 9.12, 11.9), it refers
to material want. Here it speaks of an incompleteness of faith which Paul wishes
to make good. From the remainder of the epistle (chapters 4-5) we learn in what
areas of understanding and behaviour the converts needed Paul's help—though
apparently what was lacking more than knowledge was the ability or will to apply
to their situation what they already knew.

PAUL'S PRAYER FOR THE THESSALONIANS 3.11-13

Rounding off this section and the retrospective first half of the epistle comes this
prayer, arising from verse 10, asking (a) that God would make possible a reunion
between Paul and the Thessalonians, and (b) that God would increase in the

converts brotherly love and make them 'unblamable in holiness' at the Parousia.

11. may God . . . himself: the construction suggests a contrast, though 'himself' at this stage of Greek had lost its former emphatic sense and simply here marks the opening of prayer: some contrast with Satan's hindrance (2.18) is perhaps intended.

and our Lord Jesus: grammatically this could read: 'now may God himself, both our Father and our Lord Jesus', but this would be a very unusual statement in Paul where (e.g. in 2 Th. 2.16) 'father' but not 'our Lord Jesus Christ' is generally applied to 'God'. Clearly both Father and Son are being invoked in this prayer.

direct: this verb is in the singular, which illustrates how closely in Paul's mind the Father and Jesus Christ were united. The verb used here comes in the New Testament only three times (cf. Lk. 1.79 and 2 Th. 3.5) and means 'to guide aright'.

12. The second petition which arises from the first, inasmuch as Paul seeks reunion with the converts in order to help to achieve that for which he here prays, is now stated.

the Lord: most probably, Paul means Jesus, though his prayer began by addressing both Father and Son.

make you increase: this verb is found in the New Testament only in Paul and in 2 Pet. 1.8. In 2 Th. 1.3 it is used of the converts' faith. It is to be taken (with 'and abound') with 'in love' and does not refer to numerical increase in the Christian community.

and abound: this is practically synonymous with 'make you increase': the two verbs are found together in 2 C. 4.15 as synonyms. Of the two, this verb is stronger.

in love: see on 1.3.

to one another: the love prayed for is now defined as (a) love of the brethren—the special responsibility of Christians (cf. Rom. 12.10ff.; Gal. 6.10; 1 Jn 4.7ff.), and (b) love of all men.

as we do to you: Paul not infrequently refers to his own example towards his converts (cf. 2 Th. 3.7ff.; Phil. 3.17, 4.9, etc.).

13. The prayer for the converts looks towards the desired end product.

establish your hearts: on 'establish' see 3.2, and on 'heart' see 2.4. The expression used here is found in the Old Testament (e.g. Ps. 104.15, 112.8). The prayer is repeated in 2 Th. 2.17 (cf. also Jas 5.8).

unblamable in holiness: the expression is elliptical, the sense being 'so that you may be unblamable . . .' (cf. NEB 'so that you may stand'). There are three similar words in the New Testament meaning holiness: two (*hagiotēs* and *hagiosunē*, the word used here, derived from *hagios*) refer to the possession of holiness of character, whilst the other (*hagiasmos*, derived from the verb *hagiazein*) signifies the process of becoming holy. The whole expression means here 'a holiness of character beyond reproach'.

before . . . at the coming: the point of mentioning the Parousia of Christ here is because it is then that the Christian will be seen for what he really is, just as his

4 Finally, brethren, we beseech and exhort you in the Lord Jesus
that as you learned from us how you ought to live and to please
God, just as you are doing, you do so more and more. ² For you
know what instructions we gave you through the Lord Jesus. ³ For
this is the will of God, your sanctification: that you abstain from

---

Lord will be revealed in the glory that befits him (cf. 1 Jn 3.1ff.). On 'coming', see
2.19.

with all his saints: the Greek for 'saints' is *hagioi*, 'holy ones', and it is a matter
of debate exactly whom Paul here has in mind. One possibility is that he is
referring to the angels who in the Old Testament (e.g. Zech. 14.5) as also in the
New Testament (Mk 8.38, 13.27; 2 Th. 1.7, and cf. the archangel in 1 Th. 4.16)
are expected to accompany God (in the New Testament, Jesus) at the judgment.
The real difficulty here is that Paul never elsewhere refers to angels as 'his holy
ones', though Mt. 25.31, Mk 8.38, Lk. 9.26, and Ac. 10.22 speak of 'holy' angels
(and the rabbis spoke of angels as 'holy ones'). The other possibility is that he means
'Christians' here. In favour of this it must be said that 'holy ones' in Paul's letters
means this without exception elsewhere and that this interpretation suits the context
well for Paul is speaking of *Christians* being 'holy' at the Parousia (verse 12).
Moreover, in 2 Th. 1.10 Paul speaks of Jesus coming 'on that day to be glorified
in his saints' (where he is certainly referring to Christians). Some, who incline
to this interpretation, think that Paul must be referring to *dead* Christians whom
Christ will bring with him (cf. 4.13–17) because, they say, it would be difficult
to envisage Christ 'bringing with him' the living Christians to whom he is, in
fact, coming. On the other hand '*parousia*' means 'presence' rather than 'coming'
and would allow the meaning 'at the presence in glory of our Lord Jesus Christ',
so that 'with all his saints' could suitably include dead *and* living disciples:
conceivably (with the explanation of 4.15–17 in mind) this is why Paul writes
'all' the saints. It is, on the other hand, also possible that he means 'angels and
Christians'.

(A few MSS add here 'Amen', but this is a later liturgical insertion.)

INSTRUCTION IN CHRISTIAN FAITH AND LIFE 4.1-5.22

CHRISTIAN MORALITY 4.1-12

The letter turns in this second half to exhortation and encouragement. Paul wanted
to visit his converts in order to supply what was lacking in their faith (3.10) and
(we may assume), learning from Timothy where particular help and guidance
were most needed, proceeds to instruct them by letter. For the most part it is not
new instruction that he gives (cf. verse 2) but reinforcement and application of
teaching already given.

1. Finally: this word, *loipon*, is sometimes used by Paul (as in secular Greek) to mark a transition to the closing parenetic section of his letters (2 C. 13.11; Phil. 3.1; 2 Th. 3.1). Here, as in Philippians, there is still half of the letter to come, so perhaps better than 'finally' would be 'for the rest', or, as in NEB, 'and now'.

we beseech and exhort you: 'beseech' in Greek has two meanings, the older is 'to ask', e.g. a question, and is frequently used in the sense of 'to interrogate' in the New Testament (e.g. Mt. 16.13; Lk. 9.45). The later meaning is 'to beseech' (even 'to pray') and it also is quite frequently found in the New Testament (1 Th. 5.12; 2 Th. 2.1). Coupled with 'exhort' (see on 2.11) it must here have the second meaning: 'we beg and plead' gives the combined force.

in the Lord Jesus: the expression refers here to the action of the verbs and not, primarily, to the status of Paul or of his converts (see on 2.14). It means 'in the name of', for Paul is speaking as an apostle of Christ with his authority and commission.

as you learned from us: the Greek verb is *paralambanō*, used in the early church of the transmission of the gospel message (see on 2.13), hence RV 'received' here and NEB 'we passed on the tradition'. With the exception of 4.13–18, the instruction of this part of the letter is emphatically not new (cf. 4.2, 9, 10, 11; 5.1, 2, 11).

how you ought to live: 'ought', *dei*, not infrequently carries in the New Testament a sense of divine necessity (cf. e.g. Lk. 24.7; 2 C. 5.10) and perhaps carries here something of that weight.

and to please God: see on 2.4.

you do so more and more: the Greek uses here the same verb as in 3.12, there rendered 'abound', strengthened by the adverb 'still more'; the expression is very forceful.

2. instructions we gave: repeats the meaning of 'as you learned from us' in verse 1. 'Instruction', *parangelia*, is used only here in Paul though he uses the verb not infrequently. It means an order or a precept. In the present context the latter is most fitting; 'you know what rules of conduct we gave you'.

through the Lord Jesus: Paul writes in verse 1 'we beseech you . . . *in* the Lord . . .'. Here it is 'through (*dia*) the Lord', but there is probably no significant change of meaning. In both instances Paul draws attention to his own subsidiary role and to the divine origin of his message. (For the variation between '*en*' and '*dia*' cf. e.g. 1 C. 1.10 (*dia*) with 2 Th. 3.6 (*en*).)

3. Verses 1–2 introduce this entire second half of the letter. With verse 3 we begin the first of four sections dealing with various matters of doctrine and behaviour. This one, 4, 2–12, concerns morality.

the will of God: in Greek there is no article here. In speaking of God's will Paul often includes the article, though on occasions he omits it (cf. 1 C. 1.1; 2 C. 1.1). If its absence here has significance, it is that what follows is only a part of and not the whole of the will of God.

your sanctification: the word used, *hagiasmos*, means the process of becoming

immorality; ⁴ that each one of you know how to take a wife for himself in holiness and honour, ⁵ not in the passion of lust like heathen who do not know God; ⁶ that no man transgress, and wrong his

---

perfect (see on 3.13). At the end of these instructions (5.24) Paul reverts to the same intention in a prayer. Probably 'your sanctification' is all that Paul refers to under 'the will of God': the verbs which follow ('abstain', 'know', 'not to transgress') then explicate this process of sanctification. The thought-sequence of the next few verses is: (a) abstain from fornication, verse 3; (b) take and respect a wife, verse 4; (c) do not abuse her in lust, verse 5; (d) do not by promiscuity cheat one's fellows, verse 6.

that you abstain: Paul's ethical instructions are by no means negative in tone, but he begins here with a negative command.

from immorality: 'from', *apo*, emphasizes separation and picks up the basic Old Testament meaning of 'holy', namely someone or something which, by reason of its special association with the divinity, is separated from everything profane. 'Immorality' translates the Greek word, *porneia*, meaning sexual license, any illicit sexual relationship. The question arises why Paul begins with this emphatic prohibition. Some suggest that it is because there were cases of sexual immorality amongst the Christians in Thessalonica, but it seems unlikely that Paul would have spoken so highly of his converts (cf. 3.6, 4.1) if this had been the case (see 1 C. 5.1 in contrast). Others suggest that a religious cult which included ritual orgies flourished at Thessalonica and presented a special hazard to the Christians—but the evidence for the existence of such a cult is rather tenuous. Most probably Paul begins here because the world of his time was notoriously lax in sexual matters: and at Corinth, where he writes, this was especially the case, so that Paul would be particularly aware of the need for warning in this matter. To the Jew, idolatry, fornication, and murder were the three cardinal sins, but to the Gentile, immorality was lightly regarded. Ac. 15.29 records the decision of the council of Jerusalem that less could not be required of Gentile Christians than that they abstained from fornication. This was doubtless a radical and difficult change in standards for them, and Paul not infrequently returns to the theme (Rom. 13.13; 1 C. 5.1, 6.13, 7.2; Gal. 5.19ff.; Eph. 4.17ff.; Col. 3.5).

4. Sanctification is further explained, now in a positive way.

that each of you know how to take a wife: the meaning appears to be that the Christian must honour and respect his wife, not (verse 5) allowing lust to enter into and mar his relationship towards her. But there are a number of problems of interpretation:

(i) The construction is difficult. It might be, 'to know (or respect) his wife, and to possess (supply 'her') in . . .', or it might be 'to know (supply 'how') to take a wife . . .' We cannot be dogmatic, for both are possible. In favour of the former (and against RSV) it is said that it affords all four infinitives in the Greek ('to abstain', 'to know', 'to take', and 'not to transgress') equal weight in explicating 'sanctification', whereas the latter interrupts the sequence. On the other hand the sequence is not *very* important—it is broken by verse 5, and in verse 6, there are two practically synonymous infinitives.

(ii) The meaning of 'know', *eidenai*. Some scholars think it means here 'respect', but—apart from the case of 5.12—it has in the New Testament and in classical Greek the sense 'to perceive' or 'to know how'. Almost certainly this is the meaning here, which tends to support the second construction (RSV) noted above.

(iii) The meaning of 'take', *ktasthai*. It could mean 'to acquire' or it could be 'to possess'. The former is the primary meaning and is supported by the LXX and general New Testament usage (even Lk. 21.19 probably means 'gain') and the evidence sometimes cited from papyri in favour of 'possess' is not unambiguous. Here the verb might well have both senses, 'to acquire and possess'.

(iv) The meaning of 'wife', *skeuos*. In Greek this word usually means a vessel or implement of some kind or the body as the container of a soul. Under the former sense it could be used of an inferior person, a 'chattel'. In the New Testament it is generally used of a container of some sort, though it is also used of people (e.g. Ac. 9.15; Rom. 9.21ff.; 2 C. 4.7; 2 Tim. 2.21). There is little in this to support the interpretation of some commentators (early and recent) of *skeuos* as 'body' (even 2 C. 4.7 means more than 'physical body'): but the meaning 'wife' (also favoured by some early and many recent commentators) lies nearer to hand through the sequence 'vessel'='person'=in this context 'wife'. (1 Pet. 3.7 can speak of the wife as the 'weaker vessel'.)

in holiness and honour: taking a wife is, for the Christian, part of the process of sanctification (see on verse 3) and must not interrupt or be supposed to lie outside of, this process. 'Honour', *timē*, is precisely what the heathen through their lust deny to their relationships (Rom. 1.24): it is not to be absent amongst Christians. The thought of the whole verse is akin to 1 Pet. 3.7.

5. not in the passion of lust: the contrast to verse 4. The word translated 'passion', *pathos*, comes in the New Testament only in Paul (here and Rom. 1.26; Col. 3.5) and always means overriding and illicit sexual desire. 'Lust' translates the same word as in 2.17, but here it has its usual New Testament sense of an evil desire.

like the heathen who do not know God: on 'heathen' see on 2.16. The word probably carries here its more usual sense of non-Jewish nations, for Paul will have had in mind the typically non-Jewish sexual laxity. The expression comes in LXX of Jer. 10.25 (cf. Ps. 79.6). Paul means a culpable ignorance, as in Rom. 1.28.

6. that no man transgress . . . : the thought turns from proper regard for one's wife to proper regard for one's fellow man, the sense being that promiscuity is an offence against society. The construction is a little ambiguous: it could mean, continuing directly upon verse 5, 'so that no man . . .', indicating the result of what verse 5 enjoins; more probably RSV is right in taking it as a separate clause.

brother in this matter, because the Lord is an avenger in all these things, as we solemnly forewarned you. ⁷ For God has not called us for uncleanness, but in holiness. ⁸ Therefore whoever disregards this, disregards not man but God, who gives his Holy Spirit to you.

9 But concerning love of the brethren you have no need to have any one write to you, for you yourselves have been taught by God to love one another; ¹⁰ and indeed you do love all the brethren throughout Macedo'nia. But we exhort you, brethren, to do so more

---

transgress: this word, *huperbainō*, occurs in the New Testament only here. In classical Greek it means to 'step over' and so to 'transgress'. RSV is probably right in taking the verb in an intransitive sense, though grammatically it might be taken (as 'and wrong') with 'his brother', in which case it would have to have the sense of 'transgressing against . . .'.

and wrong: Greek *pleonekteō*. It means basically 'to claim more' or 'have more than one's due', and so with an object 'to defraud'.

his brother: means 'fellow man' (cf. Mt. 5.23, 7.3f.; 1 Jn 2.9ff.) and not, in this context, only fellow Christians.

in this matter: many early Latin commentators (and some more recent scholars) refer the whole clause to covetousness, which allows a more natural meaning for the verbs used, and interpret 'in this matter' as 'in business'. But two factors weigh heavily against this interpretation: (i) although the Greek word here, *pragma*, can be used in the plural to mean 'business', it would be very unusual in the singular in this sense. (ii) Paul uses the definite article, which makes it difficult not to refer *pragma* to the subject of verse 5, namely, to gross immorality.

because the Lord is an avenger in all these things: three reasons are given in support of Paul's injunction: first, God judges offenders (verse 6); secondly, the Christian is expressly called to holiness (verse 7); and thirdly, to offend is not merely to disregard society and convention, but to disregard God (verse 8). By 'the Lord' Paul almost certainly means Jesus who, according to 2 Th. 1.8, is to 'inflict vengeance'. Probably Paul is thinking (as in 2 Th. 1.8) of the Parousia and the final judgment of transgressors, though it is possible that in a secondary sense he is thinking of the proleptic outworkings of this judgment already in history (cf. Rom. 1.24ff., 13.2ff.; 1 C. 11.30).

as we solemnly forewarned you: there are two verbs here in the Greek (as RV makes clear). The first has a temporal sense, 'told you beforehand', the second means 'solemnly testified'. Together they strongly affirm that the serious warning about immorality is no new teaching but part of Paul's exhortation at Thessalonica.

7. The second reason for moral uprightness is now given.

God has not called us for uncleanness: on 'called' see on 2.12. As in 2.3, 'uncleanness', *akatharsia*, means all forms of impurity (cf. e.g. Gal. 5.19; Eph. 5.3). 'For' translates the preposition *epi* meaning 'for the purpose of'.

but in holiness: we expect the same preposition, *epi*, to balance the negative first half of the verse, but Paul uses *en*, and the word for holiness (*hagiasmos*) which signifies the process of becoming pure; the implication is that the process of sanctification has already begun and is to continue. Romans 6.1-14 provides a commentary on this verse.

8. Therefore whoever disregards: this is the third reason for obedience. 'Therefore' looks back to verses 3-6a and is not simply the conclusion of verses 6b-7. 'Disregard', *atheteō*, means not only to overlook but positively to set aside.

disregards not man but God: 'man' is without the article and could mean man in general; but it lies nearer to hand to suppose that Paul thinks of himself—as God's messenger and apostle of Christ—and that the thought is akin to 2.13 (and cf. Lk. 10.16: whether the apostle knew this saying or not, it is a principle inherent in the term 'apostle').

who gives his Holy Spirit to you: some MSS have 'gave' (cf. AV reading), but the present tense is better attested. 'Holy Spirit' is here not in the form generally found (lit. 'the spirit of him the holy one'), but Paul is wont to vary his terms (cf. 'the spirit' in 5.19, 'holy spirit' in 1.5, 'his spirit' in Rom. 8.11). Here the stress is upon 'the holy', appropriate in the context. 'To you' is, in some MSS, 'to us' which led some early commentators to use it as a sort of proof text of ecclesiastical authority! But 'to you' is almost certainly correct here. The thought is that the process of holiness to which Christians are called is made possible by God through his holy Spirit which is given, following the death, resurrection, and ascension of Jesus, as a sort of foretaste of the End (cf. Ac. 2.16ff., and Paul's descriptions of the Spirit as *arrabōn*, 'pledge' in 2 C. 1.22, and *aparchē*, 'first-fruit' in Rom. 8.23). Anyone therefore who takes no account of the call to sanctification is setting aside not a merely human ordinance but God who makes the process possible. (The thought is akin to that of 1 C. 6.19f.)

9. Paul moves on from the demand for sexual purity to another aspect of Christian morality, brotherly love and what that involves.

love of the brethren: in 3.12 Paul spoke of 'love for all men' using the Greek word *agapē* (see on 1.3). Here, however, he uses the special word *philadelphia*, denoting, in pagan literature, family love, and in the New Testament the love which Christians bear towards each other as members of Christ (cf. Rom. 12.10; 1 Pet. 1.22). Such love is the special mark of the disciples of Christ (Jn 13,35).

to have any one write to you: the Greek is literally 'to write to you', and the sense demands the addition of such words as RSV supplies.

taught by God: this translates a single verb in the Greek found nowhere else in the New Testament or the LXX (but cf. the same thought in Jn 6.45 from Isa. 54.13). Paul is presumably thinking of the Holy Spirit who (verse 8) makes this moral behaviour possible (cf. 1 C. 2.13, 'taught by the Spirit').

10. throughout Macedonia: see on 1.7.

and more, ¹¹ to aspire to live quietly, to mind your own affairs, and to work with your hands, as we charged you; ¹² so that you may command the respect of outsiders, and be dependent on nobody.

13 But we would not have you ignorant, brethren, concerning

---

to do so more and more: the same expression as in 4.1.

11. Many commentators make verses 11–12 a separate section, but it is better to connect them closely to verses 9–10 as indicating the way in which brotherly love must express itself: it continues the exhortation begun in verse 10*b*.

to aspire: basically this verb means 'to love honour', and so it comes to mean 'to seek after honour', hence 'to be ambitious'; in later Greek it takes on the meaning 'to strive earnestly' after something. It occurs only here and Rom. 15.20; 2 C. 5.9, in the New Testament, in each instance meaning 'aspire' or 'try earnestly' (cf. NEB, 'let it be your ambition').

to live quietly: lit. to be at rest, or to be quiet. The verb is found in Lk. 23.56 of 'resting' on the Sabbath, in Ac. 21.14 it signifies cessation of an activity, whilst in Lk. 14.4 and Ac. 11.18 it means 'to remain silent'. (The adjective occurs in 1 Pet. 3.4; 1 Tim. 2.2, meaning 'undisturbed', 'unruffled', and the substantive is found in 2 Th. 3.12 meaning 'without meddling'.) The idea of inactivity is excluded here by the commands immediately following to 'do your own business and work with your hands'. The context suggests that Paul is speaking to those whose brotherly love expressed itself in busybodying and that he directs that these people should learn to behave and quietly get on with their own work. The same matter concerns Paul again in 2 Th. 3.11, where he claims to have knowledge of idlers who instead of working busied themselves in the affairs of others: it may be that Timothy had already brought back some hint of people like this in his report. A few (there can hardly have been many if the glowing praise of verse 10 means anything) thought that brotherly love could express itself in this way, and are here corrected.

to mind your own affairs: the busybodies of 2 Th. 3.11 meddled in other peoples' business. Many scholars explain this as flowing from a belief that the Parousia would certainly come within a few years: certain of this, some folk (they say) abandoned their work as pointless. But against this view it is right to notice (a) that the context here is about brotherly love, and that it lies nearer to hand to suppose that it was *this* which some Thessalonians misunderstood, supposing that, being now one 'family', they could invade their 'brethren's' privacy and also be supported by their 'brethren'; (b) that Paul's answer to them is not that, though the Parousia will indeed come shortly, they must nevertheless work, nor that the Parousia might perhaps delay and so they should work, but rather that brotherly love must not express itself in this way but in real respect for other people's privacy and real willingness to takes one's fair share in work to support oneself (this is particularly clear in 2 Th. 3.6–13, but is also clear enough here).

to work with your hands: most Christians at that time were artisans or slaves (cf. 1 C. 1.26). Unlike Jews, the Greeks rather despised manual labour. However, the emphasis is not on manual labour as opposed to some other form but upon working as opposed to idling.

as we charged you: the verb used here is stronger than 'exhort' (4.1, etc.). It signifies a really authoritative command and is used three times with reference to this matter of idleness in 2 Th. 3.6–13. Apparently Paul had given clear and definite instructions about this.

12. so that: the purpose of living quietly and working responsibly is twofold: **you may command the respect of outsiders:** lit. 'that you behave decently towards those outside'. The same words come in Rom. 13.13 (RSV 'let us conduct ourselves becomingly'). 'Outsiders' reflects a rabbinic expression and means anyone and everyone not within the Christian community (cf. Mk 4.11; 1 C. 5.12, etc.). **and be dependent on nobody:** lit. 'have need of no-one': though the Greek for 'no-one', *mēdenos*, could be masculine but could, on the other hand, be neuter. In favour of the latter, it is often remarked that the expression 'have need of' is usually followed by some *thing* (cf. Mt. 6.8; Lk. 10.42; 1 C. 12.21). It can, however, be followed by a person, as in Mt. 9.12, 26.65, and the context here suggests that Paul's concern is not that the idler will go short, but that he will make demands on his less work-shy brothers (cf. further on 2 Th. 2.6ff.).

The Dead in Christ 4.13–18

A number of scholars regard this section as the main theme of the letter, but this, we suggest, grossly exaggerates its place in the whole. The problem being dealt with here is not the supposedly unexpected death of Christians prior to the Parousia but the status of dead Christians over against living ones at the Parousia and whether (and if so 'how') those who die before Christ returns miss the first, festive phase of that event. It seems likely that Paul addresses a real situation of concern, yet it would be untrue to say that this concern arose only because he had held out to the converts the belief that none would die before the Parousia came. That Paul himself even believed that he would certainly live to see the Parousia is an open question (see below on verse 15) and it is important not to confuse the lively awareness that the Parousia could come at any moment (because 'the end' had already mysteriously happened in Christ and the open manifestation of this must be ready to occur) with an affirmation that it would certainly come within a specified time. Whilst there is much evidence to confirm that Paul held firmly to the former, evidence for the latter is very questionable.

13. we would not have you ignorant: this is an expression found not infrequently in Paul (Rom. 1.13, 11.25; 1 C. 10.1, 12.1; 2 C. 1.8), generally indicating that what follows is some teaching unfamiliar to the readers (contrast here 4.1–2, 9, 11, 5.1). The status of Christian dead at the Parousia is a matter that would arise as a problem only in the course of time; it would not be answered, nor even raised as a question, in the course of evangelistic preaching.

those who are asleep, that you may not grieve as others do who have no hope. ¹⁴ For since we believe that Jesus died and rose again, even so, through Jesus, God will bring with him those who have fallen asleep. ¹⁵ For this we declare to you by the word of the Lord, that we who are alive, who are left until the coming of the Lord, shall

---

those who are asleep: some MSS have a perfect participle, 'those who have fallen asleep', but the present is much better attested and is to be accepted. Although grammatically Paul might mean all dead people, it is certain that he means, in fact, Christian dead (cf. verse 16 'dead in Christ'; and the New Testament usage of 'sleep' in this sense is almost uniformly with reference to Christians, cf. Ac. 7.60; I C. 15.6ff., or to believers under the old covenant, cf. Mt. 27.52; Ac. 13.36; and perhaps 2 Pet. 3.4). The metaphor is found also in pagan literature and inscriptions.

that you may not grieve: this gives the purpose of the section: Paul the pastor is anxious to spare his flock unnecessary sorrow. The same thought recurs at the close of this section, verse 18.

as others: lit. 'the rest' (cf. 5.6) which means the same as the 'outsiders' in verse 12.

who have no hope: cf. 1.3. The hopelessness of the heathen found its climax in death which cast its shadow over every institution, achievement, and possession of man. (Cf. the same contrast in Eph. 2.12.)

14. Immediately we are introduced to the real problem by the answer which is given here; the Christian dead will not be overlooked but will be fully involved in all the Parousia events. The real problem is not *whether* Christians will be raised from the dead, as it *is* in I C. 15 (NEB wrongly interprets 'God will bring them to life with Jesus'), but *when* they will be raised in relation to the Parousia.

since we believe: the Greek has 'if', but the condition is expressed in the sense of a reality—'if, as we do, we believe . . .'.

that Jesus died and rose again: this is not the exact parallel of what follows (as though Paul had said 'since Christ died and rose, so will Christians die and rise') but expresses the foundation for every aspect of Christian faith and hope (cf. I C. 15.14, 'if Christ has not been raised, then our preaching is in vain and your faith is vain'). 'Died' translates the regular Greek word for dying: Paul does not speak of Christ's death as 'sleep'. 'Rose again' translates not the usual word in Paul for Christ's resurrection, and it could be that he is here recalling an earlier credal statement current in the primitive Christian communities.

even so: introducing the apodosis. The meaning is not 'if we believe Jesus died and rose, so also Christians will die and rise again', but 'because we believe . . . we can and do also believe . . .', the apodosis not being exactly parallel to the protasis, but being firmly grounded upon it.

through Jesus: there are two possible interpretations here; either 'them also that are fallen asleep in Jesus will God bring . . .' (taking 'through Jesus' with 'those who sleep'), or 'God will bring through Jesus, those who have fallen asleep' (taking 'through Jesus' with 'God will bring'), as in RV margin and RSV. The difficulty with the first alternative is that *dia*, 'through', with the genitive of a person, as here, generally means 'through the agency of', or 'on account of', which would make very awkward sense here. Some commentators explain the expression in terms of the Christian state after death which, they say, 'through Jesus' is no longer hopeless but only a 'sleep' from which they are eventually to be raised. Altogether a large number of scholars accept this first alternative. Nevertheless, the second alternative is probably to be preferred for the following reasons: (i) *dia* is given a sense much more usual and natural; (ii) the chief thought of the protasis is Jesus' death-resurrection and is balanced more appropriately by Jesus' agency in the apodosis; (iii) it is not tautologous—as some object—if the sense is 'God will bring, through Jesus . . . with Jesus'; (iv) in speaking of the Christian dead two verses later Paul uses the concise phrase 'the dead in Christ' and it seems probable that had he wished to define 'those who have fallen asleep' more nearly (the suggestion of some scholars, mentioned above), he would have used this phrase here; (v) the aorist tense suggests rather an event than a continuing state. However, the problem here is such that a dogmatic decision should be avoided and there is something to be said for the rather ambiguous RV rendering, or the repetition in NEB.

God will bring with him: the picture is of God bringing about the Parousia, being the chief agent responsible for its occurrence. This is a standpoint from which the Parousia is seldom viewed in the New Testament, though we may cf. Ac. 3.20. (The verb *agō* does not mean 'bring to life', as NEB translates.)

15. For this: refers to what follows, not to what has already been said.
declare: the Greek is the ordinary verb 'to say', and RSV 'declare' gives perhaps a solemnity not apparent in the original.
by the word of the Lord: this might mean:
(i) That Paul is citing a verse from the gospels—but the closest we have, Mt. 24.30f., is not really very close at all. (ii) That he is quoting a saying which is now lost, a not unlikely supposition, but one about which we can never be sure. (iii) That he is referring to some private revelation received in a vision (cf. 2 C. 12.1ff.; Gal. 1.12; Eph. 3.3. Ac. 21.10ff., gives an example of another person who received special revelation). This again is possible, but we cannot know. (iv) That he believes what he says to be in accord with the mind of Christ—cf. 1 C. 2.16 (and 1 C. 7.10, 12, where Paul carefully differentiates between 'word of the Lord' and his own directives, and again 1 C. 7.25, 40 where he admits to no sure revelation but believes that he speaks with 'the Spirit of God'). On (ii), (iii), and (iv) we simply cannot make a judgment since the evidence necessary for a firm decision is lacking.
that we who are alive, who are left until the coming: it is generally said that Paul certainly expected to live until the Parousia and that this verse (together with

not precede those who have fallen asleep. [16] For the Lord himself will descend from heaven with a cry of command, with the archangel's call, and with the sound of the trumpet of God. And the dead in Christ will rise first; [17] then we who are alive, who are left, shall be caught up together with them in the clouds to meet the

---

1 C. 15.51) is evidence of the fact. Sometimes this view is stated with the certainty of a proven result of New Testament criticism. But we suggest that the certainty of this idea arises more through its frequent assertion than its sound evidence. Some critics maintain that this was Paul's outlook at the time of writing his epistles to the Thessalonians, but that later he modified it. The facts appear to be: that Paul was confronted many times prior to the Thessalonian correspondence with the real possibility of being killed (cf. Ac. 9.23; 2 C. 11.23ff.); that as he writes, he knows that for himself and his converts 'waking' or 'sleeping' (5.10) were real possibilities; that in later letters, the same possibilities are still held out (cf. 2 C. 5.9 'whether at home or absent', Phil. 1.20f. 'whether by life or by death', and Rom. 14.8 'whether we live . . . or die'). Here 'we who are alive' is in fact expanded, not by 'that is to say you and I', but by 'that is to say those who are left until the coming of the Lord', the actual composition of the group being undetermined. To be sure, the perspective is that of someone who is certain that the Parousia could come at any moment (as 5.1-11 explains further), but it is not necessarily that of someone certain that he and his converts will definitely live to experience it.

'Who are left' translates a verb (perileipō) found in the New Testament only here and in verse 17. It means 'to be left over', 'to survive'.

shall not precede: Paul uses a double negative (ou mē) of great force, seldom found in the New Testament. RV captures this with its 'shall in no wise'. 'Precede' uses the same verb as is translated in 2.16 'has come' (which see), but here it has the meaning of 'come first'.

16. Having stated the answer to the problem in brief, Paul explains now how it will happen that those alive at the Parousia will in fact not enjoy some blessing denied those who beforehand have died. The picture of the Parousia here is not fuller (as is sometimes said to be the case) than that in e.g. Mk 13.24-27, but it describes other aspects. It uses imagery from Old Testament and later Jewish writing, but is notably restrained and unspeculative.

the Lord himself: certainly means Jesus, despite the perspective of verse 14.

will descend from heaven: the idea of a descent (cf. 1.10) accords with the cosmology of the time. Whether, on account of our altered cosmology, the imagery is no longer suitable or sensible, is a matter of keen contemporary debate.

Three striking events which herald the Parousia are now described. It is possible, though a little improbable, that the three expressions which follow describe one event in three ways.

with a cry of command: this translates a single Greek word used in classical literature of an order or cry, sometimes of a shouted command in battle or the word of order from a charioteer to his horses, etc. It carries a ring of excitement, activity, urgency, and authority. It is found nowhere else in the New Testament. Paul gives no indication who it is who shouts and the whole description is such that we ought, probably, to leave the details as vague as he presents them.

with the archangel's call: lit. 'a voice of an archangel'. The only New Testament archangel named is Michael (Jude 9), but the absence here of the definite article suggests Paul had no particular angelic being in mind. Rev. 1.10, 4.1 mention a voice like the sound of a trumpet; perhaps this combination of ideas is what led Paul on to the next expression.

with the sound of the trumpet of God: cf. Mt. 24.31; 1 C. 15.52. In the Old Testament the trumpet accompanied the spectacular theophany of Mount Sinai (cf. Exod. 19.13, 20.18) and is expected to sound on the 'Day of the Lord' (Isa. 27.13; Zech. 9.14; etc.). It also features in apocalyptic writing.

And the dead in Christ: on the expression 'in Christ' see 2.14. Paul means those who through faith have aligned themselves with Christ's death and resurrection and who have died in this faith. In 1 C. 15.23–26, he gives a similar picture of the order involved in the general resurrection, whilst the writer of Revelation has an elaborate picture of two resurrections (Rev. 20.5ff.). Here the Christian dead are explicitly mentioned because it is precisely *their* position at the Parousia that seems to have been a problem to the converts at Thessalonica.

will rise first: the same verb is used as in verse 14, though a few MSS change this to Paul's more usual word (*egeirein*). 'First', means before the living Christians are caught up to meet Christ, verse 17.

17. we who are alive: see on verse 15.

shall be caught up: this verb, *harpazō*, means to snatch away, suggesting violence and haste (cf. Mt. 11.12, 13.19; Ac. 8.39; 2 C. 12.2, 4; Rev. 12.5). The thought, as in 1 C. 15.51, is that those remaining alive until the Parousia will not pass through death, yet their situation will nonetheless be radically altered.

together with them: an unusual expression in the Greek (occurring again in 5.10) meaning here 'simultaneously, with them'. The affirmation of verse 15 is repeated.

in the clouds: in the Old Testament 'cloud' is part of the imagery of theophany, signifying God's presence and emphasizing the mystery of it (Exod. 13.21, 16.10, 19.9, etc.). Cloud also formed part of the stock imagery describing the expected Day of the Lord (cf. Ezek. 30.3; Dan. 7.13; Jl 2.2) and features in the New Testament in a similar context (as here and cf. Mk 13.26; 14.62; Rev. 1.7; etc.). Paul intends to stress the majesty and awe of the occasion.

to meet the Lord: there is some evidence to suggest that the verb 'to meet' (Paul uses the substantive here) was connected in contemporary Greek language with the reception accorded to royal visits. However, it is quite probable that

Lord in the air; and so we shall always be with the Lord. ¹⁸ Therefore comfort one another with these words.

5 But as to the times and the seasons, brethren, you have no need to have anything written to you. ² For you yourselves know well that the day of the Lord will come like a thief in the night. ³ When people say, 'There is peace and security,' then sudden destruction

---

Paul means here simply 'encounter' without any special overtones.

in the air: in late Jewish literature, 'air' was thought to be the abode of spirits and to be generally antagonistic to man (cf. Eph. 2.2). But Paul can use the word in a neutral sense (1 C. 9.26, 14.9), and it is doubtful if he means here more than 'space'. What happens after this event, whether Christ and 'the saints' descend to earth or ascend to heaven, is not dealt with here, and Paul is not concerned to give a systematic account of the End. Sufficient is said to answer the problem presented, and no more.

so shall we always be with the Lord: having met Christ, the living and the formerly dead Christians are never again to be parted from him. This declaration forms a fitting conclusion to the whole matter (and again, whether this involves judging with him, reigning with him or simply 'being' with him, is irrelevant to the matter in hand and is therefore avoided).

18. comfort one another: as Paul indicated in verse 13, his concern for the converts in this matter was more than an academic interest in the answer to their problem, and at the close of this section he returns to the same thought. On 'comfort' see 'exhort' in 2.11 which translates the same Greek word, though in this context the emphasis is on comfort and encouragement.

PREPARATION FOR THE PAROUSIA 5.1–11

Unlike 4.13–18, but similar to the rest of this second half of the letter, Paul speaks in 5.1–11 of things already familiar to his converts. The purpose of the section is to encourage the Thessalonians to fuller commitment and stronger obedience. What he would have attempted in person had he been present, he seeks to do by letter in his absence. There is no suggestion (as some maintain) of a crisis in the church, nor even of a problem, but Paul would be aware of the constant need under any circumstances for exhortation and pastoral care if slackness and apostasy were to be avoided.

1. the times: cf. on 2.17. This translates the Greek word *chronos*, chronological time.

and the seasons: translates *kairos*, which in the New Testament means especially God's propitious moments for special redemptive acts. Together, these two words embrace all questions about when, how long before, how suddenly or how heralded, the outstanding redemptive event, the Parousia, will occur (all the topics included in the disciples' question in Mt. 24.3; cf. Ac. 1.7).

to have anything written to you: here the verb is in the passive, so RSV rightly supplies 'anything' (which is lacking in the Greek); contrast 4.9.

2. you yourselves know well: 'well' renders a Greek adverb (*akribōs*) used by Paul only here and in Eph. 5.15 (there translated 'carefully'). In classical Greek it means 'accurately', 'precisely', and this is its sense elsewhere in the New Testament (cf. Mt. 2.8; Lk. 1.3; Ac. 18.25, 23.15, 20, 24.22). Some, finding it difficult here, suggest that Paul is replying to a letter from Thessalonica and giving them credit for accurate knowledge at this point. Others suggest that he means that they know accurately a word of Christ's on this matter (e.g. Mt. 12.39). But the adverb can have its straightforward sense here of 'accurately' and simply mean that Paul is assured (by Timothy?) that the converts know exactly what Paul had taught them about the end coming suddenly and about the need to be prepared.

the day of the Lord: this expression is found in the Old Testament from the Book of Amos (5.18, 20) onwards, often abbreviated to 'that day'. It was envisaged variously, but altogether three particular events were expected through the Lord's (or his special representative's) presence: judgment of the nations, blessing of the righteous, and the restoration and renewal of all things by the overthrow of evil. Paul is by no means uniform in his terms, speaking at times of 'that day' (2 Th. 1.10), 'the day of our Lord Jesus' (2 C. 1.14), 'the day of Christ' (Phil. 1.10), 'the day of Jesus Christ' (Phil. 1.6).

will come: the Greek uses the present tense which not only gives vividness to the thought but aptly expresses something of the New Testament insistence on the nearness of the Parousia. This nearness, we suggest, is based upon the tension (already spoken of, see on 1.10 and 2.12) involved in the redemptive events, a tension between past accomplishment in the mystery of Christ's life, death, and resurrection, and awaited consummation in the open manifestation of Christ's Parousia. It is expressed in a variety of ways in the New Testament (e.g. 'the end of the times', 1 Pet. 1.20; 'in the last days', 2 Pet. 3.3; 'upon whom the end of the ages has come', 1 C. 10.11; 'the Lord is at hand', Phil. 4.5; the end comes 'quickly', Rev. 22.7, 12, 20). It should not be mistaken for a belief that the End would certainly come within a delimited period, a belief which, we suggest, is not part of the teaching of the New Testament nor of the faith of the early church as a whole.

like a thief in the night: the same picture comes in 2 Pet. 3.10 and Rev. 3.3, 16.15, though 'in the night' is found only here (being omitted in the best MSS of 2 Pet. 3.10). The idea of suddenness, which this vividly portrays, is expressed in other ways in the New Testament, in e.g. Mt. 24.42–51, 25.1–13; Mk 13.33–36. Always it is closely connected with a call to watchfulness.

3. The idea of suddenness and unexpectedness is now developed from the standpoint of those who are unprepared.

will come upon them as travail comes upon a woman with child, and there will be no escape. ⁴ But you are not in darkness, brethren, for that day to surprise you like a thief. ⁵ For you are all sons of light and sons of the day; we are not of the night or of darkness. ⁶ So

---

When people say: a general hypothetical clause with which the emphatic 'but you' in verse 4 contrasts.

'There is peace and security': this is reminiscent of Jer. 6.14; Ezek. 13.10; Mic. 3.5. It is also, presumably, what the householder says to himself as he leaves his house unattended (Mt. 24.43). The word translated 'security', *asphaleia*, is found in the New Testament only here and in Lk. 1.4; Ac. 5.23. The direct style can be rendered as reported speech, with RSV, or paraphrased as in NEB 'when they are talking about peace and security'.

then sudden destruction: those who do not reckon with the coming of the Parousia possess a false security which will be rudely shattered. 'Then' corresponds with 'when' earlier. The word for 'sudden', *aiphnidios*, is—like 'security' earlier—a word found in the New Testament only in Paul and Luke. Luke (21.34) also uses the word in connection with the End coming upon the unprepared. 'Destruction', *olethros*, can mean in Greek 'ruin', 'destruction', or 'death'. The same word is used in a similar context in 2 Th. 1.9 (elsewhere in the New Testament only in 1 C. 5.5 and 1 Tim. 6.9), which passage suggests that the destruction envisaged is to be understood as 'exclusion from the presence of the Lord' (see further on 2 Th. 1.9).

will come: translates another infrequent New Testament word, used here as also sometimes in this mood in classical Greek of coming suddenly in a hostile sense. It is in the present tense, as 'will come' in verse 2 (which see).

as travail comes upon a woman with child: imagery found not infrequently in the Old Testament (cf. Isa. 13.8; Jer. 6.24; Hos. 13.13; etc.). The point of the comparison is the inescapability of the destruction for those unprepared, hence the verse concludes by making this explicit.

there will be no escape: 'And they shall in no wise escape' (RV) is more exact and stresses the emphatic negative (*ou mē*, on which, see 4.15). This is possibly another echo of Lk. 21.34–36.

4. The purpose of recounting this negative side of the Parousia hope is to exhort the converts to watchfulness and preparedness to which Paul now (verses 4–8) turns.

But you: the emphatic 'you' contrasts with the general 'people' in verse 3.

not in darkness: fastening upon the idea of the Parousia as 'the day' and upon the thought that to the unprepared it comes as 'a thief in the night', Paul now develops the theme in the current symbolic contrast of light with darkness. He means more than 'you are not ignorant', or 'you are not blind' (cf. Rom. 2.19).

Darkness here (and generally in the New Testament, cf. Lk. 22.53; Rom. 13.12; Col. 1.13; etc.), has eschatological significance. Paul likens the present world to the sphere of darkness (cf. Eph. 6.12; 2 C. 6.14) out of which Christ has already delivered the believer (Eph. 5.3; Col. 1.13); the 'light', which properly belongs to God's kingdom, to 'the day of the Lord', has already appeared in Jesus Christ (cf. 2 C. 4.6) and those who are aligned with him through faith already share in that light and are to take on its character by ethical obedience (verses 6-8, and with this passage cf. Rom. 13.12f.; 2 C. 6.14f.; Eph. 5.1ff.).

for that day to surprise you: participation in the light of the approaching day through faith in Christ is the first requisite for the Day not to come upon one unawares. Paul is going to develop the idea of preparedness in terms of the ethical obedience proper to this participation (verses 6ff.) but only on this necessary foundation. 'Surprise' renders the Greek *katalambanō*, here (as in Jn 12.35) meaning 'to overtake'.

like a thief: here, as in Rev. 3.3, it is explained that the thief metaphor is applicable only to those who do not watch and are unprepared. To those who reckon with the Parousia's coming, it will not be a rash, calamitous shock. A few MSS have 'for that day to surprise you like thieves', which some commentators prefer because, they argue, this could easily have been altered to the other less offensive reading, but hardly vice versa. However, 'like a thief' repeats the expression in verse 2, and could easily have been altered accidentally (*kleptēs* to *kleptas*); further-more the accepted reading is much better attested.

5. For you are all sons of light: this is the positive expression of what Paul meant in verse 4 by 'you are not in darkness', and is thoroughly eschatological. It means more than 'light is your character' although 'sons of', 'children of' is a Semitism which can mean 'characterized by' (cf. e.g. 1 Pet. 1.14; Eph. 2.2); it means here, 'you belong to the kingdom of light, inasmuch as you belong to Jesus'. The expression is found in Lk. 16.8 and it also occurs in the Dead Sea Scrolls (where it features prominently in the Manual of Discipline and in the Wars of the Sons of Light against the Sons of Darkness).

and sons of the day: the thought is very similar to 'sons of light', only now the new situation brought about by Jesus' advent is viewed in terms of 'day'. Christians, by faith in Jesus Christ, already belong to 'the day', i.e. the Day of the Lord, already belong to the realm that will, in that Day, be revealed.

we are not of the night: Paul reverts to the first person plural, emphasizing the missionaries' solidarity with the converts in not belonging to the realm of darkness (on which see verse 4). 'Night' and 'darkness' signify more than opposition to God, for they refer to the whole era and realm of wickedness ('this world' as Paul sometimes calls it, cf. Rom. 12.2; 1 C. 2.6, 8; 2 C. 4.4; Gal. 1.4; etc.) which, in a hidden and mysterious way, has been overthrown by the appearance of Christ (cf. esp. Eph. 1.20ff.; Col. 2.15), and though its power enjoys in the present a 'last fling', it will be manifestly put down by the appearance of Christ in glory at the End.

then let us not sleep, as others do, but let us keep awake and be sober. ⁷ For those who sleep sleep at night, and those who get drunk are drunk at night. ⁸ But, since we belong to the day, let us be sober, and put on the breastplate of faith and love, and for a helmet the hope of salvation. ⁹ For God has not destined us for wrath, but to

---

Paul not infrequently turns to the first person plural when he enters upon exhortation presumably, in part, so as not to appear to 'lord it' over those to whom he writes, and also, in part, because he was well aware of his own need to persevere (cf. Phil. 3.12).

6. So then: i.e. because we belong to the new era, the 'day of the Lord' which has come and is to come. Paul uses a strong expression, *ara oun*, which appears also in 2 Th. 2.15.

let us not sleep: the verb used here, *katheudō*, (different from that in 4.15, 17) can mean ordinary physical sleep (as in verse 7), or the sleep of death (verse 10) or, metaphorically, the life of those who belong to the realm of darkness (as here). It is used by Paul only in this passage and in Eph. 5.14 (and it is the word describing the disciples' slumber in Gethsemane which evoked the command 'watch and pray, that ye enter not into temptation', Mt. 26.41). For Paul, not only the past events of Jesus' death and resurrection evoke and demand ethical obedience (Rom. 6.5ff.; Gal. 2.20; Col. 3.1; etc.), but also the coming Parousia encourages and demands the same (Rom. 13.12ff.; 1 C. 6.9f.; Eph. 5.1-14; etc.).

as others do: (cf. on 4.13) i.e. those who delude themselves with a false security (verse 3), who belong to the realm of night and of darkness.

but let us keep awake: this, like 'sleep', above, is reminiscent of Mt. 26.41, and the thought is closely akin to the parable of Mk 13.34-37 (cf. also Lk. 12.37; Ac. 20.31; 1 C. 16.13; Col. 4.2; 1 Pet. 5.8; Rev. 3.3). The verb *grēgoreō*, means 'to watch', 'to be vigilant', and signifies the proper attitude of the Christian in this time between Ascension and Parousia.

and be sober: the word used here could, in Greek, mean 'not under the influence of drink', but it is obviously used here in a metaphorical sense. It denotes serious, responsible moral behaviour as drunkenness denotes abandonment of self-control and responsibility. We may notice that the wicked servant in the parable of Mt. 24.45-51, abandoning his watchfulness, is said to 'eat and drink with the drunken'. The same conjunction 'watch and be sober' occurs in 1 Pet. 5.8, there coupled (unlike here) with the thought of temptation ever ready to strike.

7. The theme of this verse is that immoderate and immoral behaviour belong to the realm of night and darkness but are quite inappropriate to the realm of light and day. The verse reads almost like a marginal gloss (which some, with insufficient evidence, have supposed it to be).

who get drunk are drunk: two related verbs are used here as synonyms. The usage is best explained as a matter of style.

8. since we: 'we' is emphatic, contrasting with those 'others', verse 6, who sleep and are drunken. 'Since' rightly gives the note of causality intended in the Greek.

belong to the day: this confirms that Paul in verse 5 means more than 'you have the character of light', and that he is speaking all the time eschatologically. Paul believed that God had 'delivered us from the dominion of darkness and transferred us to the kingdom of his beloved Son' (Col. 1.13).

let us be sober: 'sober' is, in this passage, sufficiently a synonym for 'watch' that Paul repeats only the one word from the expression used in verse 6.

and put on: two thoughts now converge. The one is that the Christian must arise and dress himself because it is day-time (cf. Rom. 13.11–14); the other is that in his attempt to watch and prepare for the Parousia, the Christian is menaced by temptation (cf. Mt. 26.41; 1 Pet. 5.8), and needs to be armed. Participation in the events of Christ's life, death, and resurrection is referred to a number of times as 'putting on'—'Jesus Christ' (Rom. 13.14); 'the new man' (Eph. 4.24); 'a heart of compassion' (Col. 3.12).

the breastplate of faith and love: the image of donning a breastplate and helmet goes back to Isa. 59.17. The Christian life is here thought of as a fight (cf. also 1 C. 9.26; Eph. 6.12; 1 Tim. 6.12; 2 Tim. 4.7), for which the Christian requires his armour (Rom. 13.12; 2 C. 6.7; Eph. 6.11). The suggestion that Paul is thinking of the great struggle with Antichrist is rather improbable though, of course, the Christian life is a struggle only because the realm of darkness and night, overcome in principle, continues to wield a limited power. On the triad faith, love, and hope which reappear here, see 1.3. Whilst faith is grounded in the past events of salvation history, and hope strains towards that which is still to come, love spans the two, looking back to its mainspring (cf. 1 Jn 4.19) and forward to its consummation (cf. 1 C. 13.12f.).

for a helmet the hope of salvation: 'salvation' is, according to Paul, the content of the gospel (Rom. 1.16); it is that which God in Christ has accomplished independently of and for mankind; it is also the present appropriation of this by faith; and it is the eventual revelation of God's gracious work in Christ at the End. Since salvation is connected here with hope, it is this future aspect which is to the fore.

9. For God has not destined us: the reason for the Christian to fight and hope is nothing less than the fulfilment of a divine purpose that he should be saved. God's purpose is viewed first in its negative aspect, for salvation is first of all salvation *from* wrath. The verb translated 'destined', *etheto*, means originally 'to put' or 'place' and is often so used in the New Testament. Occasionally, however, it has the purposive sense which it bears here (cf. 1 Tim. 1.12; 2 Tim. 1.11; 1 Pet. 2.8). Paul does not enlarge on this theme here (see on 1.4).

for wrath: see on 1.10. Though the primary thought is of 'wrath to come', Paul

obtain salvation through our Lord Jesus Christ, [10] who died for us so that whether we wake or sleep we might live with him. [11] Therefore encourage one another and build one another up, just as you are doing.

[12] But we beseech you, brethren, to respect those who labour

---

probably means here that the Christian is not destined either to participate now in wrath or to be the recipient of wrath at the last.

but to obtain salvation: God's purpose is now viewed from the positive side. 'To obtain' (lit. 'for obtaining') translates a word, *peripoiēsin*, found seldom in the New Testament (or outside it) which presents difficulties. It can mean 'preservation,' 'a possession', 'obtaining', or 'acquiring'. The problem is, does Paul mean here 'God has set us for obtaining salvation', or 'God has set us for preservation to salvation', or 'God has set us for a possession of salvation'. We cannot be certain. But 'to obtain' would seem to accord best with the sense of the whole passage, parallel to 'obtaining wrath', and also seems to be the sense intended in 2 Th. 2.14. 'Salvation' might well now (contrast verse 8) have a broader reference than simply the future, as we suggest 'wrath' also has here.

through our Lord Jesus Christ: strictly speaking, the instrumentality of Christ might refer back to God's determining action, though the immediate reference is to 'salvation'; if the ambiguity is not intentional, it is certainly fortuitous.

10. The primary theme of verses 9–10 runs as follows: 'God has not destined us for wrath, but to obtain salvation through our Lord Jesus Christ, who died for us so that we might live.' Into this Paul has introduced a secondary thought, reverting to the problem discussed in 4.13–18: this thought is, 'whether we wake or sleep, we might together be with him'.

who died for us: Paul is well aware that the crucifixion and the resurrection together achieve salvation for mankind (Rom. 4.25; 1 C. 15.17; etc.), but the title here 'our Lord Jesus Christ' indicates well enough that it is the *risen* Jesus of whom it can be said 'he died for us' and so Paul adds no explicit statement of the resurrection. Paul offers no explanation in these epistles as to *how* Christ's death was vicarious, nor why. This is because there was, in the matters under discussion in these letters, no occasion or necessity to do so (contrast Rom. 5.12–21; 2 C. 5.14–19, etc.). It does not indicate that Paul had as yet not developed this theme in his mind nor already included it in his preaching. Indeed, the affirmation of the vicarious ('for us') death of Christ in this almost passing manner suggests that it must have been well understood by the converts.

so that whether we wake or sleep: those who understand 4.15, 17 as meaning that Paul certainly expected to be alive until the Parousia tend to overlook this verse, where Paul appears to reckon with two possibilities both for himself and for his converts. The metaphorical usage of 'sleep', though employing the same word as in 5.6, 7, goes back to the theme of 4.13–18 and refers to death. Similarly 'being awake' here does not mean 'not sleeping' in the sense of 5.6, but indicates the possibility of being still alive at the Parousia.

we might live with him: the object of Christ's death (and resurrection) is that we might live; this explicates the short-hand term 'salvation' in verse 9. On 'with him', see 4.17. The reference is primarily to the future; the verb is an aorist which suggests an event rather than a process, here the event at which dead and living Christians will meet the Lord and always be with him (4.17).

II. This section closes as did the previous one with an exhortation to use what Paul has written as a pastoral help.

encourage: see on 2.11.

build one another up: the verb used here, *oikodomeō*, is the regular one for building a house (as e.g. in Mt. 7.24ff.; Lk. 4.29), but it is often used in the New Testament in a metaphorical sense—by Jesus of his church (Mt. 16.18) and by Paul of the Christian community (Eph. 2.22) or of individual Christians (as here). In this verse it carries the sense of growing through deepened understanding. Paul uses two ways of expressing 'one another' in this verse but without essential difference.

just as you are doing: there is no need to suppose that Paul is merely being polite. The praise he accords his converts in 1.6ff., 2.13f., and 3.6 indicates that he is here stating no more than the truth.

Various Precepts 5.12–22

Completing this second half of the epistle comes a section of pastoral guidance where it seems that the Apostle's mind ranges over the broad area of church life and Christian service. There is no need to see behind each injunction a special situation supposedly requiring particular guidance; much of the advice and encouragement is of a general character such as Paul would regard right and necessary for any church, particularly a newly established one, in its everyday life and work.

12. Verses 12–13 concern the relationship of the congregation to its appointed officers. It is possible that some of the leaders amongst the converts had been tactlessly officious and it is possible that some of the congregation had been resentful of guidance or rebuke (the Macedonians were noted for their spirit of independence). It is, however, equally possible that Paul mentions this matter because it was, as it remains, a constant source of misunderstanding and difficulty in any church.

we beseech you: marking a new section. See on 4.1.

respect: lit. 'know', the same verb as Paul uses in its usual sense in 1.4 ('we know'). There seem to be no cases of its usage with the meaning 'respect' anywhere else in the New Testament, nor in classical Greek (Paul uses in 1 C. 16.18 another verb for 'to know', with the meaning 'to respect'). Perhaps NEB 'acknowledge' is more exact.

among you and are over you in the Lord and admonish you, [13] and to esteem them very highly in love because of their work. Be at peace among yourselves. [14]And we exhort you, brethren, admonish the idle, encourage the faint-hearted, help the weak, be patient

---

those who labour among you: as there is one definite article and three participles, Paul is indicating a group of people and not three particular officers. He first describes their work as labour, then expounds what this entails in two other participles. If we are to believe Ac. 14.23, it was the practice very early in the church's life to appoint elders, *presbuteroi* (after the pattern provided by Jewish synagogues), and it is natural to assume that this had happened, despite the missionaries' hasty departure, at Thessalonica (perhaps they are 'Jason and certain brethren' who were dragged by the Jews before the civic authorities and from whom surety was taken (Ac. 17.6ff.)). Some scholars think that at this early stage in the church's life the office of elder had not evolved. However this may be, Paul had clearly in mind here a group who had special pastoral responsibilities and functions. 'Labour' (see on 1.4, where the substantive is used) denotes hard work in a quite general sense.

are over you: the Greek verb used here, *proïstēmi*, has a variety of meanings but its basic sense is 'to set over'. It could be used of voluntary, informal leadership (which is the sense accepted here by those scholars who think there were at this time no elders), but it could also denote an official leader or office-bearer. The word, in this sense, is not altogether devoid of a note of superiority, which is probably why Paul adds to this participle 'in the Lord', giving to the secular word a unique quality.

in the Lord: this can hardly mean here that those who are put over the converts are themselves 'in the Lord', i.e. are fellow-Christians, for this would go without saying. Paul is referring to the authority which those who labour in the church hold and exercise. They are the commissioned servants of Christ and are therefore 'over' the converts in the very special sense in which Christ was 'over' his disciples (see Mk 10.42–45; cf. 2 C. 4.5). The distinction and the unique honour of the Christian leader is to be the servant of the congregation 'over' which he is set. Church government and ecclesiastical hierarchy must always bear this special character of being 'over' the laity 'in the Lord' and should certainly not abandon this in order to model its functions and structure upon the state or any other system of management and discipline.

and admonish you: lit. 'to put you in mind', hence 'to advise' or 'to warn'. The verb is found in the New Testament only in Paul and Ac. 20.31. The note of serious yet loving admonition which Paul probably here intends is evident in its use in 2 Th. 3.15.

13. to esteem them: in the New Testament the Greek verb used here, *hēgeomai*, usually has the meaning 'to count', 'to deem' (it occurs, for instance, in 2 Th. 3.15, translated 'look on'). Somewhat like 'know' in the previous verse, this verb acquires its special nuance here in virtue of what follows.

very highly: this, and what follows, qualifies the verb. It signifies the degree to which the converts are to regard their leaders. The adverb is very strong; see on 3.10 ('earnestly').

in love: on *agapē*, see 1.3. This signifies the manner in which the leaders are to be regarded.

because of their work: this gives the reason for which the leaders are to be highly regarded. Paul does not explain more narrowly why their work merits the converts' high esteem, so we may assume that he is speaking in a general sense. The work they do is perhaps well done; it is certainly necessary, certainly arduous; it is essentially service of God and also service of the converts themselves; it is part of the furthering of the gospel upon which Paul places always great weight.

Be at peace among yourselves: it is possible that Paul had knowledge, through Timothy, of some particular trouble among the believers at Thessalonica, but again this is the sort of admonition that an experienced pastor would write independently of any special crisis or problem. It probably does not belong to the next section (as NEB supposes), but follows from what Paul has said about due regard for the leaders. 'Live peaceably', which is the sense intended (cf. Mk 9.50; Rom. 12.18), involves a due regard for those who lead and a due tact and care from them.

14. Verses 14–15 concern pastoral care and discipline.

And we exhort you brethren: it is tempting to think that Paul here turns to the leaders, giving them special advice and encouragement (to 'admonish', 'encourage', 'help', and 'be patient' would presumably be their special tasks). But grammatically it would be very difficult to give to 'brethren' a different reference here than it has in verse 12, and the expression 'we exhort you, brethren' can hardly, after 4.1, 4.9, and 5.12, suddenly mean a particular group within the total community. It is probably right, therefore, to assume that Paul regards the whole congregation as in some sense involved, with its leaders, in the care and nurture of the community.

admonish the idle: on 'admonish', see on verse 12. 'The idle' probably refers in the first instance to those apparently being spoken of in 4.11 (which see, and cf. 2 Th. 3.6ff.) who took advantage of their fellows, trading on their brotherly love. The Greek word *ataktos* really means 'not in battle-order', signifying a soldier who steps out of line or who has deserted his post. From this it comes to mean, generally, 'disorderly'. There is, however, evidence in the papyri that it can denote unwillingness to work, or absenteeism. The conjunction in 4.11 of the two commands 'mind your own affairs' and 'work with your hands' suggests that we are to think of some who, through idleness, busied themselves in other people's affairs and were, so to speak, 'out of step' as Christians.

encourage the fainthearted: 'encourage', *paramutheomai*, only here and in 2.11 (which see). 'Fainthearted' translates a word found only here in the New Testament (though it comes a number of times in the LXX). Here it means 'timid'. If

with them all. 15 See that none of you repays evil for evil, but always seek to do good to one another and to all. 16 Rejoice always, 17 pray constantly, 18 give thanks in all circumstances; for this is the will of God in Christ Jesus for you. 19 Do not quench the Spirit,

---

we recall that the Thessalonian church was a 'church under the cross' (cf. 1.6) we can well understand that some of the converts needed encouragement to overcome trepidation. The reference may also be to the problem dealt with in 4.13–18, some converts growing discouraged because of their fears that some Christians were to be excluded from full participation in the Parousia. (There is, however, no suggestion here, as some maintain, of discouragement in the face of a supposedly unexpected delay of the Parousia.)

help the weak: Paul elsewhere has not a little to say about the responsibilities of the 'strong in faith' towards those who are weaker (cf. 1 C. 8.7–13; Rom. 14.1–6). 'Spiritual weakness' is most probably what Paul has in mind, though it would be true to say that he would have also encouraged support for the physically and materially weak and impoverished (cf. his own diligent provision for the material needs of the Jerusalem churches (cf. Ac. 24.17; 1 C. 16.1; Gal. 2 10)). The verb 'support' is not a common New Testament one; in classical Greek it means 'to stand one's ground', 'to hold out against', but in the New Testament it has the sense 'to cling to' (Mt. 6.24; Tit. 1.9), as here. 'Hold firmly the weak ones' gives the meaning.

be patient with them all: RSV (and NEB) apparently interprets those towards whom patience has to be exercised as the three groups already mentioned (idle, fainthearted, and weak), patience being the manner in which the admonishing, encouraging, and helping is to be carried out. But 'towards all' is possibly to be taken in a wider sense; patience is to be shown not only towards the three groups mentioned, but towards everyone else as well. 'All' then has the same connotation as in verse 15. 'Patience', *makrothumeō*, is strictly 'long-suffering' and, like the other New Testament word for patience, *hupomonē* (see on 1.3) means not a negative acquiescence but a steadfast, active perseverance.

15. See that none of you: the Greek has 'see that no one . . .' in the third person, as though Paul is advocating keeping an eye on others so that they do not offend in this way. But the change to the third person is almost certainly a matter of style only, and RSV rightly retains the sense in continuing the second person.

repays evil for evil: the same expression occurs in Rom. 12.17 and 1 Pet. 3.9 whilst the thought is to be found in Mt. 5.44. As an ideal it is also to be found outside the New Testament, but in the New Testament it is established as the negative side of Christian behaviour on the ground of Christ's own example (cf. 1 Pet. 2.19ff.).

but always seek to do good: this is the positive side of Christian moral behaviour.

'To do good' is all-embracing and means much the same as is meant in Rom. 13.10, 'love does no wrong to a neighbour'. 'Good' here is not some abstract, philosophical ideal, but the active, steadfast attempt to promote the well-being of one's fellow men.

16. Verses 16-22 are injunctions concerning the individual Christian's right behaviour. First Paul gives a threefold command relating to his basic attitude in life.

Rejoice always: on 'rejoice' see 1.6 ('joy'). The Thessalonians had already suffered (cf. 1.6, 2.14, 3.3f.) but had 'received the word ... with joy inspired by the Holy Spirit' (1.6) despite such troubles. Paul exhorts to constant rejoicing because that which evokes joy, namely the truth that 'God raised Jesus from the dead ...' (1.10), is incomparably greater than transitory afflictions. To the Philippians, also enduring afflictions, he writes similarly (Phil. 4.4, and cf. on the same theme Rom. 5.3ff.; 2 C. 12.10; Col. 1.24, for a rationale of rejoicing through sufferings).

17. pray constantly: on 'pray' see 1.2. Clearly, Paul could not mean that the Christians should spend their whole time saying prayers (he has already told them to get on with their work! 4.11). 'Prayer' in this context is rather the constant sense of dependence upon God and the unwillingness to wrestle with a problem or need independently of him (cf. Paul's own example, 3.10). This injunction is found also in Rom. 12.12; Eph. 6.18; Col. 4.2.

18. Give thanks in all circumstances: the third of the triad of injunctions concerning the Christian's bearing. On 'give thanks' see on 3.9. 'In all circumstances'—not quite the same as 'always' (verse 16) or 'without ceasing' (verse 17); though meaning 'at all times', it draws attention to something of the paradox of Christian thanksgiving, even in situations ostensibly regrettable.

for this: grammatically the last injunction only might be the subject of 'this', but it is more likely that Paul means all three commands (verses 16-18) for although 'this' is singular it can refer to the three commands regarded as a unity.

is the will of God: on 'will of God', see 4.3.

in Christ Jesus: God's will is expressed and perceived in the life, death, and resurrection of Jesus Christ and in him the promises of God are, as it were, signed and sealed (cf. 2 C. 1.20).

19. Verses 19-22 concern spiritual gifts. The Spirit who authenticates the gospel message (1.5), who inspires joy in affliction (1.6), who makes possible the holiness to which Christians are called (4.8), also manifests his presence in various abilities (cf. 1 C. 12.4-11), some of which tended, in the early church, to foster disorder or contention.

Do not quench the Spirit: the verb, *sbennumi*, 'to put out', is used because the Spirit is likened to fire (cf. Ac. 2.3). The gifts of the Spirit are, indeed, to be incorporated in an orderly and peaceable fashion into the life of the church, serving the whole community (cf. 1 C. 14.1-19), but the Spirit himself is not to be restrained or extinguished. The negative, *mē*, with a present imperative (and not an aorist subjunctive) indicates that the Thessalonians were in fact guilty of doing this;

²⁰ do not despise prophesying, ²¹ but test everything; hold fast what is good, ²² abstain from every form of evil.

23 May the God of peace himself sanctify you wholly; and may

---

it is not just a warning for the future. In view of the command which follows, 'do not despise prophesying', it would seem best to understand by 'Spirit' here, utterances inspired by the Spirit, perhaps ecstatic utterance 'in tongues'. The two injunctions together then correspond to 'by spirit or by word' of 2 Th. 2.2 (cf. 1 C. 13.8 'as for prophecy, it will pass away; as for tongues, they will cease'). To interpret 'Spirit' as the 'fruits of the Spirit' (Gal. 5.22) as, for instance Chrysostom did, leaves verse 20 isolated.

20. Do not despise prophesying: prophets are highly regarded in the New Testament (cf. 1 C. 12.28; Eph. 2.20, 3.5, 4.11). According to 1 C. 14.3 'he who prophesies speaks to men for their upbuilding and encouragement and consolation'. It is there likened to 'speaking in tongues' except that no interpretation is needed; indeed it is direct exhortation (cf. also Ac. 15.32). It is most likely this general character that Paul has here in mind, rather than prediction which is one particular aspect of prophesying (cf. Ac. 11.27f.). There is no evidence to support the view that some at Thessalonica had predicted a particular date for the Parousia and, because it had not come and the prediction had proved wrong, prophesying had been brought into disrepute. More likely, a natural independence of spirit tended to lead the Thessalonians to ignore the utterances (ecstatic or direct) of those who sought to encourage them and build them up in faith (cf. verses 12–13 above).

21. test everything: a number of scholars believe that Paul has in mind here a saying known to the early church and which might have been a word of Jesus himself which ran, 'be approved money-changers' (or 'bankers'), the adjective 'approved' being from the same root as the verb here 'test'. Against this, however, it must be noted that the verb 'test', *dokimazō*, was current in Greek, was well known in the LXX, and is used earlier in this letter (2.4 'approved'), and that in the absence of any evidence more substantial a link with this unrecorded word, perhaps of Jesus, is extremely tenuous. If the thought continues what Paul has to say in verses 19–20, it is likely that Paul means 'scrutinize all manifestations of the Spirit's gifts holding to what is good and rejecting what is not'. This is, then, the positive side (cf. the adversative 'but' at the outset) of the negative injunctions of verses 19–20. (Later in the church's life, the problem of discerning between good and bad prophets, genuine and false apostles, honest preachers and mere charlatans became quite grave, and in the Didachē we find this advice on the subject: 'Let everyone who comes in the Lord's name be received; then when you have scrutinized him (*dokimazō*) you will know him . . . and if he wishes to stay with you and is an artisan then let him work and eat; if he has no trade, of your wisdom devise how he might live as a Christian—not in idleness—with you. If he will not do this, he is making a trade of Christ; beware of such.')

hold fast what is good: 'hold fast' translates Greek *katechō*, a word with its problems in 2 Th. 2.6-7. It has in classical Greek a variety of meanings. In the New Testament it is used most frequently meaning 'to hold fast' (e.g. Lk. 8.15; 1 C. 11.2, 15.2; Heb. 3.6; etc.), though it also appears meaning 'to possess' (e.g. Lk. 14.9; 1 C. 7.30) and 'to restrain' (e.g. Lk. 4.42; 2 Th. 2.6). Here, as one side of the result of testing, it means to retain and accept. 'Good', *kalos*, is not the same word as in verse 15 (*agathos*), but is practically synonymous. It is the opposite of the 'evil' of verse 22.

22. abstain from every form of evil: apparently a reminiscence of Job 1.1, 8. 'Abstain' in Greek, though meaning the opposite of 'hold fast' in verse 21, has a very similar form; the English 'retain . . . abstain' would give a comparable effect. 'Form', *eidos*, might here mean 'appearance' (as RV margin), or 'kind', 'sort'. If we are right in verse 21 in thinking that Paul means 'scrutinize all manifestations of the Spirit's gifts', then Paul could mean here 'abstain from every evil manifestation', i.e. those which after testing are found not to be genuine. But there may be a wider and more general reference, in which case NEB 'bad of whatever kind' will be correct. RSV 'form' allows for both possibilities. 'Evil', *poneros*, has a variety of meanings in the New Testament ranging from 'wilful' (Mt. 7.17) through 'harmful' (Mt. 5.39) to positively wicked (Phil. 3.2; etc.); the great adversary of man could be described as 'the evil one' (Mt. 13.19; Eph. 6.16) and the character of the present age summed up in the expression 'this present evil age' (Gal. 1.4; cf. Eph. 5.16). At times it is uncertain whether 'the evil' refers to the 'evil one' or to the evil at work in the world (cf. e.g. Mt. 6.13; 2 Th. 3.3).

CONCLUSION 5.23-28

The letter is now drawn to a close. As the first half ended with prayer (3.11-13), so this second half, and with it the whole letter, is concluded with prayer.

23. May the God of peace himself: 'himself' and the Greek particle *de* (omitted by RSV, NEB; rendered 'and' in RV) suggest a contrast between what is now asked of God and what was before exhorted of the converts. 'God of peace' is not uncommon at the conclusion of Paul's letters (cf. Rom. 15.33, 16.20; 2 C. 13.11; Phil. 4.9; 2 Th. 3.16). In 1 C. 14.33 God is referred to as a God of peace in order to buttress Paul's efforts to restore order to the confusion in the church's worship there. But it is unlikely that Paul uses the expression in closing his letters for any such purpose. Rather, he uses peace in its fullest sense, and stresses that God is the God of the entire process of salvation, the God who makes peace between himself and the world (Rom. 5.1) and between man and man (Eph. 2.14). See on 1.2.

sanctify you: Paul rarely uses the verb, but does so here (on 'sanctification' see 3.13 'holiness'). Here it is God who sanctifies; in Eph. 5.26 it is Christ who sanctifies his church, and in Rom. 15.16 sanctification (the verb here is in the passive) is achieved through the Holy Spirit. The holiness which Paul enjoins (4.3ff.) is attainable only through God's action, therefore it is first and last to be prayed for

your spirit and soul and body be kept sound and blameless at the coming of our Lord Jesus Christ. ²⁴ He who calls you is faithful, and he will do it.

25 Brethren, pray for us.

26 Greet all the brethren with a holy kiss.

27 I adjure you by the Lord that this letter be read to all the brethren.

28 The grace of our Lord Jesus Christ be with you.

(cf. 3.13 and here): it is God who will do it (verse 24).

wholly: *holoteleis*, a word found only here in the New Testament, and rarely in classical Greek. It means 'quite completely' and is here explained in what follows as complete perfection at the last.

may your spirit and soul and body: controversy has existed from the early church Fathers until today whether Paul subscribed to a dichotomous or to a trichotomous view of man. Here it might seem that he held the latter, whereas in 1 C. 7.34 he presents us with a view which seems to support the former. However, Paul is here not expounding anthropology (nor indeed is he in 1 C. 7.34 !) but is engaged in praying, and his prayer is that his converts in every particular, in their wholeness as human beings, may be kept sound.

'Spirit', *pneuma*, is, according to 1 C. 2.11, that part of man where resides his capacity for self-knowledge. Unlike the Stoics, Paul has no dualism of 'good' spirit and 'bad' body; spirit can be referred to man in his sin (Rom. 11.8)—though it happens that Paul generally speaks of 'spirit' in a good sense.

'Soul', *psuchē*, is more or less in Paul's usage the 'life principle'; in Rom. 11.3 (a quote from 1 Kg. 19.10) it means 'life' in contrast to death. It does not feature frequently in Paul.

'Body', *sōma*, on the other hand, is very frequently used, sometimes in a non-moral sense (e.g. Rom. 4.19), in many cases falling under condemnation (e.g. Rom. 7.24); it can, however, be redeemed (Rom. 8.23). (Paul also speaks of 'flesh', *sarx*, generally denoting man's proneness to sin; 'mind', *nous*, refers to man's reasoning faculty, capable of perversion by 'the flesh', but also of renewal by God; and 'heart', *kardia*, generally that with which man thinks, feels, and wills, or 'the whole man'.) For a discussion of these terms in Paul see R. Bultmann, *A Theology of the New Testament*, London, 1952, Vol. 1, pp. 191–246.

be kept: has a sense of protecting, watching over, and guarding.

sound: this word is in the singular, confirming that 'spirit, soul, and body' are regarded as one unit, the whole man. In the Old Testament it is used of the 'unhewn' stones to be used in building God's altar. In Philo and Josephus it is used of the unblemished state of sacrificial animals; and in Wisdom (15.3) it refers to moral integrity.

and blameless: see on 3.13.

at the coming of our Lord Jesus Christ: as in 3.13, the Parousia is seen as the time when the process of sanctification will be made manifest and its results assessed. It is then that the Christian will be seen for what he is and his works revealed in their true light (cf. Mt. 25.31-46).

24. He who calls: present tense, as in 2.12 (which see). The unexpressed subject is 'God'.

is faithful: not infrequently Paul mentions the faithfulness of God in the context of prayer (here and 2 Th. 3.3; also 1 C. 1.9, 10.13; 2 C. 1.18; cf. also 2 Tim. 2.13; Heb. 10.23, 11.11). 'Faithful' in this context is objective, meaning that God is trustworthy.

and he will do it: lit. 'and he will do' (reminiscent of the saying in Num. 23.19, 'hath he said, and shall he not do?', and cf. Mt. 23.3). Paul is confident that 'he who began a good work (in you) will bring it to completion at the day of judgment' (Phil. 1.6, which is a good commentary on the crisp expression here). Rom. 8.28ff. further elaborates God's entire oversight and initiative in the salvation events. We note that Paul never affirms God's oversight in these matters as an excuse for idleness but as the reason for the convert to have confident hope.

25. Pray for us: this is no mere politeness, but an earnest request. Elsewhere (Rom. 15.30ff.; Eph. 6.19; Col. 4.3, and 2 Th. 3.1) his prayer requests are more particular, always connected with his ministry, but here the request is left vague. (Some MSS add *kai*, 'pray also for us', which might be original and is virtually the sense anyway.)

26. all the brethren: Paul means to be all-inclusive and there is no reason to see in 'all' (contrast 'one another', verse 15) a hint of estranged members or of a divided church!

a holy kiss: (cf. also Rom. 16.16; 1 C. 16.20; 2 C. 13.12; 1 Pet. 5.14). By about A.D. 150 the kiss of peace was a regular feature of the central liturgical service of the church, the Eucharist. It came after an exhortation to be reconciled one with another (a 'proof-text' sometimes cited in this connection being Mt. 5.23f.), and was the sign and seal of amity and unity. It led, later, to certain abuses and died out in the Western rite in the Middle Ages. Whether this is what Paul refers to here or not is a matter of uncertainty; it seems probable that the letter would have been read at the Eucharist (see on verse 27) and it is possible that the kiss of peace had a place in that service from earliest times. 'Holy' kiss might be more appropriate as a reference to this liturgical pledge of peace than to a sort of friendly greeting (as e.g. in Lk. 7.45).

27. The first person singular occurs again here and it is possible that the final verses (probably verses 25-28) were added by Paul with his own hand, as was generally his custom (cf. 1 C. 16.21; Gal. 6.11; Col. 4.18; 2 Th. 3.17).

I adjure: this verb, *enorkizō*, is a stronger form of the usual word, *horkizō* (found in Mk 5.7; Ac. 19.13). It is very emphatic and means 'I put you on oath to . . . .'.

by the Lord: cf. 'by God' in Mk 5.7 and 'by Jesus whom Paul preaches' in Ac. 19.13. Probably 'Lord' here means Jesus.

that this letter be read: i.e. when the congregation is met together for its worship, this letter is to be read aloud. Various reasons have been offered why Paul insists on this being done, some thinking that he feared the letter might be misused (cf. 2 Th. 2.2) and that this was his way of guarding against that possibility, others maintaining that the church at Thessalonica was deeply divided (see Introduction, p. 15) and that this is Paul's way of ensuring that his letter reaches everyone. However, in Paul's great desire to return to the church at Thessalonica (2.17f., 3.1, 10) to continue his work there we have reason enough for this command; his letter is nothing less than a substitute for a personal visit and is intended to accomplish all that a visit would have done; *therefore* it must be read to all.

(A few MSS add 'holy' to 'brethren', but probably through a mistake in transmission. Paul never elsewhere uses such an expression.)

28. Paul closes all his letters with such a benediction as this, sometimes shorter (as in Col. 4.18), sometimes expanded (as in 2 C. 13.14; Eph. 6.24). On 'grace', see on 1.1. (The addition in some MSS of 'Amen' is from a later hand, as are also the subscriptions 'written from Athens' and 'written from Corinth'.)

THE SECOND LETTER OF PAUL TO THE

THESSALONIANS

THESSALONIANS

1 Paul, Silva′nus, and Timothy.
To the church of the Thessalo′nians in God our Father and the Lord Jesus Christ:

2 Grace to you and peace from God the Father and the Lord Jesus Christ.

3 We are bound to give thanks to God always for you, brethren, as is fitting, because your faith is growing abundantly, and the love of every one of you for one another is increasing. 4 Therefore we ourselves boast of you in the churches of God for your steadfastness and faith in all your persecutions and in the afflictions which you are enduring.

THE ADDRESS 1.1–2

The address differs from that in the first epistle in only two particulars. (1) Here Paul speaks of God as 'our' Father, whereas in 1 Th. 1.1 he is 'the' Father, and so 'the Father of Jesus Christ'. Here he is 'the Father of believers' (Rom. 8.14–17 enlarges on this theme). (2) 'From God the Father and the Lord Jesus Christ' is added after the salutation 'grace to you and peace'. This then becomes the standard practice in all epistles (though Colossians has simply 'from God our Father' in some MSS, several important authorities add 'and the Lord Jesus Christ'). The close association of Father and Son at this early date is noteworthy (the Greek preposition 'from' is not repeated, Father and Son being treated as a single source of grace and peace).

2. Some important MSS have 'from God *our* Father . . .' as in every other epistle of Paul's; it could well be original, though RSV omits.

PERSEVERANCE IN AFFLICTION 1.3–12

THANKSGIVING FOR THE THESSALONIANS' FAITH 1.3–4

As in the first letter, Paul begins by expressing gratitude to God for his converts' growing faith. In this letter he has matters to put right and faults to correct, but that does not diminish the apostle's recognition of progress and achievement in the church.

3. We are bound: cf. also in 2.13. Some commentators regard the tone here as cold in comparison with 1 Th. 1.2; but 'we are bound' does not indicate a grudging acknowledgment but a personal debt; cf. NEB 'our thanks are always due to God'). Paul means simply, 'we owe it to God'.

to give thanks: see on 1 Th. 1.2.

as is fitting: this does not repeat the sense of 'we are bound' but adds the new thought that this thanksgiving is also appropriate in the circumstances, since the Thessalonians have really progressed in their Christian faith and life. It is possible, as some commentators suggest, that Paul's praise in the first letter had created an impression of flattery, or had provoked the reply from the converts that he was overpraising them; to this he now answers, 'not at all; thanks are both due and appropriate'. (*Axios*, the word used here, generally means in the New Testament 'worthy', but is found in 1 C. 16.4 with the meaning it takes in this verse, 'appropriate in the circumstances'.)

your faith: Paul here mentions faith and love as the objects of his thanksgiving, whereas in 1 Th. 1.3 he added 'steadfastness of hope'. But in the next verse he mentions 'steadfastness' as one of the reasons for his 'boasting', so the thought of patience and hope is not far from his mind.

is growing abundantly: this verb, *huperauxanō*, is found only here in the New Testament. The growing faith is, in a sense, the answer to Paul's prayer in 1 Th. 3.10.

and the love of every one ... is increasing: this is, to some degree, the answer to Paul's prayer in 1 Th. 3.12. The apostle emphasizes that this love is shown 'by each one of all of you', which NEB renders well, 'each for all and all for each'.

4. we ourselves: the construction marks something of an emphatic contrast perhaps over against the Thessalonians who made no claims for themselves, or more probably over against the apostle's former silence (cf. 1 Th. 1.8 'so that we need not say anything'). 2 C. 8.1ff. is an example of such boasting.

boast: Paul uses here a compound form of *kauchaomai* (see on 1 Th. 2.20), found only here in the New Testament and only four times in the LXX. It is here practically synonymous with the more usual form.

in the churches of God: this must mean more than in Corinth alone and could mean in fact 'all the churches throughout the world', but probably it has much the same significance as the expression in 1 Th. 1.7, 'the believers in Macedonia and in Achaia'.

steadfastness and faith: because of the conjunction of these two words and the fact that in the Greek there is a single article, 'faith' is understood by some to mean here 'faithfulness'. But faith seldom has this sense in Paul's writings (see on 1 Th. 1.3) and in the previous verse almost certainly means 'conviction and commitment'. Faith, as continual commitment to the gospel, is here made an object of boasting just because, like perseverance, it is most difficult to maintain in adversity and affliction.

persecutions: this word, *diōgmos*, is more often than not in the New Testament linked, as here, with other expressions of suffering (e.g. in Mt. 13.21 with 'tribulation'; in Rom. 8.35 with 'tribulation and distress'; in 2 C. 12.10 with 'distress', and

5 This is evidence of the righteous judgment of God, that you may be made worthy of the kingdom of God, for which you are suffering—⁶ since indeed God deems it just to repay with affliction those who afflict you, ⁷ and to grant rest with us to you who are afflicted, when the Lord Jesus is revealed from heaven with his mighty

---

in 2 Tim. 3.11 with 'affliction'). Here the word, though almost synonymous with 'afflictions' (on which, see 1 Th. 1.6), draws attention to the actual attacks which brought affliction as a consequence.

you are enduring: the present tense indicates that trouble did not end for the converts with the expulsion of the missionaries, though we have no exact knowledge of what happened in Thessalonica after that.

THE OUTCOME OF AFFLICTION 1.5-10

Paul now gives something of a rationale of suffering. The whole section is thoroughly eschatological. It has two parts: verses 5-7a concern the principles of judgment and verses 7b-10 relate to the occasion and manner of judgment.

5. This is evidence: i.e. a sure token and sign. The problem is to know what Paul means by 'this'; is it (1) steadfastness and faith, or (2) persecutions and afflictions, or (3) steadfastness and faith through persecutions and afflictions? We must return to this later in the verse.

the righteous judgment of God: the righteous judgment of God is not an abstract principle nor a law of nature but an eschatological event ('the Great Assize'), already enacted in Jesus' death and resurrection and one day to be openly revealed in the Parousia of Christ (see on 1 Th. 1.10). In the present time, and 'in faith' man can already appropriate the objective acquittal achieved by Christ for man (cf. Rom. 4.25). In this sense it is the converts' faith that is the token of the judgment of God, evidence that at that judgment the converts receive his verdict of acquittal.

that you may be made worthy of the kingdom of God: on 'kingdom' see 1 Th. 2.12. Like judgment, this kingdom has come in the life, death, and resurrection of Jesus, but will also be openly revealed only at the Parousia. The verb used here, *kataxioō*, means 'to account worthy' rather than 'to render worthy', and the thought is still upon the verdict of acquittal at the 'Great Assize' to which faith lays claim. At the same time this verb draws attention to the need for *real* faith in contrast to an unworthy lip-service or a self-justification (cf. Mt. 7.21ff.). In this sense, it is the steadfastness and continual conviction and commitment of the converts in the face of opposition that is the token of the verdict of acquittal to be pronounced at the End. Faith is attested as *real* faith in such an affiliation to Christ as agrees to suffer with him (cf. Rom. 8.17; Phil. 1.28f.), as agrees to 'lose his life' for Christ's sake and the gospel's (cf. Mk 8.34f.).

We suggest that by 'this evidence' Paul means the steadfastness and faith which endure through persecution, which point towards the End judgment of God and which lay claim to the verdict of acquittal already secretly enacted but at the Parousia to be openly proclaimed. There seems to be little to support the suggestion of some that Paul means by 'this', 'the fact that their faith lasts despite opposition shows that God is helping them' (though, of course, Paul attributes his converts' perseverance to God's grace, cf. verse 3).

for which you are suffering: i.e. 'for the sake of which', or 'in the name of which'. The thought is akin to Mk 8.35 'for my sake and the gospel's. The Greek here adds *kai*, 'for which *also* you are suffering', hinting at Paul's own afflictions at Corinth at the time of writing (cf. further verse 7, 'rest *with us* to you').

6. since indeed: renders a rhetorical introduction (*eiper*) which allows of no contradiction of what follows.

God deems it just: 'just' refers still to the Great Assize and to the eschatological event of judgment referred to in verse 5.

to repay with affliction: the verb used here is found in the Old Testament with reference to God's repayment of Israel's enemies (cf. Isa. 59.18, 66.6; etc.). 'Affliction', *thlipsis* (see on 1 Th. 1.6), denotes here the eschatological distress to be poured out at the End upon the enemies of God, though it does not exclude the thought that this distress is already, proleptically, being meted out (cf. further in chapter 2).

those who afflict you: the repayment of affliction with affliction is precisely the principle of the *lex talionis* of Lev. 24.40 (cf. similarly in Lk. 16.25; Col. 3.25; Rev. 13.10). Some commentators find the thought here so 'Jewish' as to show, they think, that the passage is non-Pauline; but Paul's teaching is not that God has suddenly turned his back on the *lex talionis* but that its consequences have been vicariously enacted in Christ. Furthermore, the principle of judgment is now so bound up with the person of Christ that, as verses 7-8 expound, vengeance is to be outpoured upon those who have rebelled against God not in any general or vague sense, but in the specific sense that they have rejected Christ; just as those who receive 'rest' are not those who have achieved enough merit, but those who are 'in Christ'.

7. The first half of this verse gives us the positive aspect of the divine principle of judgment.

To grant rest: 'rest', *anesis*, is found in Paul's epistles meaning physical and mental calm (cf. 2 C. 2.13, 7.5). In classical Greek it could refer to the release of a bow-string, and so comes to mean relaxation and recreation generally. In the context of this passage it means 'eternal rest' which, in turn, must be understood in terms of 1 Th. 4.17, 'so we shall always be with the Lord'. (The idea of salvation as 'rest' is expounded in Heb. 3-4 on the basis of Ps. 95.7ff.)

with us: i.e. because we too believe and our faith is attested as genuine faith through endurance of affliction.

when the Lord Jesus is revealed: verses 7b-10 form the second part of this section on the outcome of suffering, describing the occasion and manner of

angels in flaming fire, ⁸ inflicting vengeance upon those who do not
know God and upon those who do not obey the gospel of our Lord
Jesus. ⁹ They shall suffer the punishment of eternal destruction and
exclusion from the presence of the Lord and from the glory of his

---

judgment. Affliction and rest will be meted out when Jesus is 'revealed', i.e. at the
Parousia (on which, see 1 Th. 2.19). 'Revelation', *apokalupsis*, draws attention to
the fact that the Parousia is to be an unveiling, an open unambiguous manifestation
of the true glory of Jesus Christ in contrast to his presence in humility and hiddenness in his earthly life and his presence in the equivocation and limitations of his
church. (Verbs of seeing are frequently used in the New Testament in connection
with the future coming of the Kingdom and of the Son of Man; cf. Mt. 24.33,
26.64; Mk 9.1, 13.26, 14.62; etc.).

The description of the Parousia in verses 7*b*–10 is suspected by some of being
non-Pauline (either a Jewish little apocalypse used by Paul, or an early Christian
hymn). It is quite rhythmic in form and has many allusions to Old Testament
passages, but neither fact is reason enough to say that it is not from Paul's own
hand.

from heaven: cf. 1 Th. 1.10, 4.16.

with his mighty angels: in the Old Testament angels serve as the messengers of
God and, especially in later writings, serve to enhance the sense of mystery and
majesty surrounding God (cf. e.g. Isa. 6.2ff.). In the New Testament they appear
especially where human experience reaches its bounds (cf. e.g. Mt. 1.20; Jn 20.12),
and therefore are frequently mentioned in connection with the Parousia (cf. Mt.
13.39, 41, 16.27, 24.31, 25.31). 'Mighty' renders the Greek word *dunamis* and could
mean, as RSV, NEB, and AV understand, 'mighty angels', treating the genitive
substantive as an adjective (a common Semitism). On the other hand, *dunamis* in
the eschatological context of Mk 14.62 is a circumlocution for the divine name;
taken as a substantive here 'his power', with reference to Jesus, could be Paul's way
of referring to Jesus' divinity, that which is to be openly manifested at the Parousia;
Jesus is to be revealed with angels appropriate to and underlining his divine nature.

in flaming fire: RSV (with NEB) rightly links this to verse 7 and the description
of the appearance of Jesus in glory (rather than, as RV, taking it, as the start of
verse 8, in connection with 'inflicting vengeance'). 'Fire' is used as a figure of divine
judgment in the Old Testament (cf. e.g. Isa. 66.15; Dan. 7.9) and in the New
Testament (cf. e.g. Mt. 25.41; Mk 9.43, 48; 1 C. 3.13ff.; Jude 7; and cf. the thought
of a world conflagration in 2 Pet. 3.7). Fire also expresses something of the majesty
and power of God's presence (cf. Exod. 3.2; Rev. 1.14). So Paul's description here
speaks of movement (from heaven), accompaniment (with his angels) and surrounding (in fire).

8. inflicting vengeance: judgment is to occur at the Parousia, as verse 7 explains. This verse enlarges on the manner in which judgment is to be meted out. The expression 'inflicting vengeance upon those who do not know God' is reminiscent of Ps. 79.6; Jer. 10.25.

those who do not know God: it is possible that Paul means two groups of people who fall under God's judgment: (1) those who do not know him and (2) those who do not obey the gospel. But it is far more likely that the two clauses are virtually synonymous, in the manner of Hebrew parallelism, and that the latter expounds the former. On the expression 'do not know God', see on 1 Th. 4.5. 'To obey' the gospel means the same as 'to believe', but draws attention to belief as submission (cf. Rom. 6.16–23).

9. The construction of this verse is, like verse 8, most probably based on the idea of parallelism; 'punishment of eternal destruction' is enlarged by a practically synonymous expression 'exclusion from the presence of the Lord', the latter part of which is itself expanded by another synonymous phrase, 'from the glory of his might'.

They shall suffer: the verb (*tinō*) means to pay a price by way of recompense, or to pay a penalty. It is found only here in the New Testament.

punishment: the Greek word, *dikē* (only here and Ac. 28.4, Jude 7), originally signified what is right and just, and then comes to mean the process of deciding what is right, i.e. a law-suit or trial; it then takes on the meaning of a punishment or payment following a trial. Here it has this last sense. Those who have afflicted the followers of Christ (verse 6) and disobeyed the gospel (verse 8) must now pay the penalty.

eternal destruction: see on 1 Th. 5.3. The word 'eternal' (*aiōnios*) is used here with the thought-world of the Old Testament in mind, where 'eternal' characterizes something of the quality of God's existence and purposes which defy description in ordinary, temporally restricted terms. The word has a meaning which is neither 'timeless' nor even 'everlasting'. Likewise in the New Testament 'eternal life' is not life outside a time-scale nor is it simply life going on for ever; it is life which flows from God and from fellowship with him (cf. Jn 3.15f.; Rom. 6.23; etc.). Here it is the exact opposite that is referred to, 'eternal ruin', a desolation which proceeds from God's righteous judgment and which therefore must share in the 'supra-temporal' quality of his life and of all his decisions.

exclusion from the presence of the Lord: there is no word in the text for 'exclusion' which reads, 'who shall suffer destruction . . . from the face of the Lord and from . . .'. The problem here is, what does 'from' (*apo*) mean? There are three possibilities: (1) it means 'exclusion from', as RSV, NEB make explicit in their translations. (2) It means 'proceeding from', which is what RV could be taken to imply. (3) It means 'from the time of', i.e. *at* the presence of the Lord. On the two latter views, the expression defines the source or moment of punishment, whereas on the first view it is a further description of the punishment itself. On the whole the first view seems preferable in view of the contrasting reward of the 'saints' which is spoken of in verse 10.

might, 10 when he comes on that day to be glorified in his saints, and to be marvelled at in all who have believed, because our testimony to you was believed. 11 To this end we always pray for you, that our God may make you worthy of his call, and may fulfil every good resolve and work of faith by his power, 12 so that

---

The expression 'from the presence of the Lord and from the glory of his might' is practically a quotation from Isa. 2.10. There it is a description of sinful man before the majesty of God; here it is of sinful man before the glorified and manifested Christ.

10. when he comes: the indefinite *hotan* with an aorist subjunctive denotes a single event at an unspecified future date.

on that day: practically this is a technical term from Old Testament imagery for the final revelation of God at the end of time (cf. Isa. 2.11; Jer. 4.9; Am. 2.16; etc.; and in the New Testament, Mt. 24.36, 26.29; 1 Th. 5.4; etc.). The sense of this verse is made clearer by RSV bringing this phrase forward from the end, where it comes in the Greek (and in RV), to this position.

to be glorified in his saints: Paul uses here and in verse 12 a verb, *endoxazō*, which occurs nowhere else in the New Testament (though it is found in the LXX in e.g. Isa. 49.3). The thought here may be that as Jesus appears in glory, this glory will be reflected in his followers who will be caught up with him (cf. similarly 1 Jn 3.2): this takes 'in' in a local sense. On the other hand, if we take 'in' in an instrumental sense, Paul could mean that as Christ appears his followers will worship him, rendering him the glory due to him. The latter sense seems to be suggested by the meaning of the less ambiguous expression following. On the other hand, the former sense gives a better parallelism with verse 9—some are to be transformed into the likeness of Christ in his presence, whilst others are to be excluded from his presence. But perhaps both possibilities were in mind and it is not necessary to choose between them.

On 'saints' see on 1 Th. 3.13.

and to be marvelled at: the parallelism in this passage, verses 7b–10, continues, for this clause is practically synonymous with the preceding one. 'To be glorified in' is now unambiguously the wondering adoration of the beholders of the glorified Christ, and 'his saints' is now explained as those who have believed in Christ (the aorist tense is used, indicating one decisive event which might be the initial, decisive act of faith in turning to the gospel in the first place, or might be the whole life of faith viewed, from the standpoint of the Parousia, as a single event. In view of the expression which follows, probably the former alternative is the right one).

because our testimony to you was believed: Paul's mind has not wandered from the actual situation of the converts in Thessalonica, though he has been describing the Parousia scene, and he now picks up the theme of verse 5 that the believer already lays claim to the verdict of acquittal 'at that day' by faith. The construction is elliptical, but the sense is clear. Paul reminds the converts that they will be amongst the glorified and glorifying saints, the 'marvelling believers', because they responded to the missionaries' preaching. 'Testimony', *marturion*, which takes the concrete form of preaching, is emphasized in The Acts as the primary responsibility and function of the apostles (cf. Ac. 1.8, 22, 2.32, 3.15, 5.32; etc.) and Paul can speak of his preaching as 'the testimony to Christ' (1 C. 1.6). 'To you' renders the Greek *epi*; in Lk. 9.5 'witness' with '*epi*' means witness *against*, but here the sense is of a witness accosting the Thessalonians (and there may even be a hint of the adverse circumstances (cf. 1 Th. 2.2) attending Paul's preaching at Thessalonica).

PRAYER 1.11–12

As so often happens (cf. 1 Th. 3.11–13; 2 Th. 1.11f., 16–17) Paul closes a section with a prayer. Having just declared that by their response of faith the Thessalonian converts have laid claim to be amongst those who welcome and worship Christ at his Parousia, he now prays that this faith may prove to be *real* faith through holiness in life.

11. To this end: this means, with NEB, 'with this in mind'. The prayer has in view the Parousia and the judgment, but also the immediately preceding thought of the converts' initial response of faith.

make you worthy: a similar verb to that in 1.5 is used meaning, usually, 'to count' worthy rather than 'to render' worthy, although in fact the stress here may well fall on the latter idea. The thought is probably 'that God may account you worthy by making you worthy by fulfilling every good resolve . . . .'.

his call: in 1 Th. 4.7 God's call is thought of as a past act whilst in 1 Th. 2.12 and 5.24 it is a continuous event. It is often discussed whether or not Paul indicates here the possibility of his converts' falling away from faith; what is certain is that the converts can only be accounted and rendered worthy through the grace of God (verse 12) and through faith being attested as genuine faith, again by the power of God (verse 11*b*)—for which things Paul deems it necessary to pray.

to fulfil: not here in the sense of filling up or completing (as e.g. in Mt. 13.48; Phil. 4.18), but in the sense of accomplishing (as also e.g. in Mt. 3.15; Ac. 12.25).

good resolve: lit. 'the good resolve of goodness' (cf. RV margin), which is a little awkward. AV inserted 'his' and made 'goodness' refer to God. RSV and NEB take 'goodness' as reinforcing 'good resolve', probably rightly. The prayer is that God will bring to effect the good intentions which he puts into the minds of Christians ('goodness', *agathōsunē*, is itself a fruit of the Spirit, cf. Gal. 5.22; Eph. 5.9).

work of faith: cf. on 1 Th. 1.3. Paul does not mean works inspired by faith (as NEB) but the outworking of faith which is itself real faith as opposed to spurious 'lip-service'.

by his power: this is the equivalent of an adverb qualifying the action of the verb

the name of our Lord Jesus may be glorified in you, and you in him, according to the grace of our God and the Lord Jesus Christ.

2 Now concerning the coming of our Lord Jesus Christ and our assembling to meet him, we beg you, brethren, [2] not to be quickly shaken in mind or excited, either by spirit or by word, or by letter purporting to be from us, to the effect that the day of the

---

'fulfil'; hence RV 'with power' and NEB 'mightily bring to fulfilment'. (There is no 'his' in the text, but clearly it is the divine power which Paul means.)

12. so that: the prayer of verse 11 has as its purpose the ultimate end of Jesus being glorified by his followers and the followers sharing in the glory appropriate to Jesus: this intention is partially realizable in the present but can only be consummated at the Parousia (cf. 1 Th. 3.13, 5.23).

the name of our Lord Jesus: 'name' generally in the New Testament is used with the same significance as in the Old Testament, i.e. meaning the person to whom the name belongs (cf. e.g. 'hallowed be thy name', Mt. 6.9).

may be glorified in you: as in verse 10, there is some ambiguity here. Paul might intend us to understand 'in' in a local sense, 'in your worshipping presence at the Parousia', or he may intend 'in' to signify manner, 'Christ will be glorified as his splendour is reflected in your transformed presence'. In view of the phrase 'and you in him' the latter sense is to be preferred.

and you in him: i.e. by union with Christ the Christians share in his glory (cf. Jn 17.10, 22). This is true as a present reality, but only in a very partial and limited sense. It will be true in a complete and unambiguous sense only when Christ appears in glory at his return.

according to the grace: Paul's prayer acknowledges that what he desires for the converts can be accomplished only by divine favour, favour in accord with the supreme act of divine bounty, the life, death, and resurrection of Jesus Christ. On 'grace' see 1 Th. 1.1.

our God and the Lord Jesus Christ: the Greek has 'our God and Lord Jesus Christ', so grammatically 'God and Lord' could both refer to Christ; but more likely Paul is referring to both Father and Son.

THE MYSTERY OF LAWLESSNESS 2.1–17

In this chapter, Paul tackles a problem which had apparently arisen, or was in danger of arising, in the Thessalonian community, concerning the coming of the Parousia. We must not exaggerate the dimensions of this problem for there is no evidence that it had reached anything like a crisis. Furthermore, the causes leading to the problem are not obscure; Paul's message was that the eschatological event had in a sense already occurred, but in a mystery, in Jesus Christ's life, death, and resurrection; already the blessings of the End could be appropriated by faith and the End anticipated in faith-union with Christ. In tension with this was his conviction and sure hope that the eschatological event would yet occur in an open and unambiguous form, still bound up with the person of Christ but Christ no longer in hiddenness and humility but Christ glorified. It always lies close to hand to dissolve this tension either through a loss of serious hope in the Parousia, or through failure to appreciate the real purpose for which the present interval between resurrection and Parousia is given, namely in order to allow time and opportunity for the gospel to be preached and for men to repent and believe.

Exegesis of this chapter must proceed with special caution since it is amongst the most disputed of Paul's writings.

The Problem 2.1–2

I. Now ... we beg you, brethren: see on 1 Th. 4.1.

the coming: Greek *parousia*, presence. See on 1 Th. 2.19.

our assembling to meet with him: this is the aspect of the Parousia spoken of in 1 Th. 4.14ff. and again in 2 Th. 1.10. The noun 'assembling together', *episunagōgē*, is found in the New Testament only here and in Heb. 10.25, where it refers to Christians assembling for worship, especially with an eye on the approaching Parousia. The assembling here is 'to him' (*ep auton*), which RSV understands as motion towards and so 'to meet with him'.

2. not to be quickly shaken in mind: the verb in its literal sense refers to being tossed about by wind or storm (cf. e.g. Mt. 11.7; Lk. 6.48), but it is used here in a figurative sense (as also e.g. in Ac. 17.13 of 'stirring up' trouble). By the aorist tense, the suddenness of the shock is emphasized. 'Mind' (see on 1 Th. 5.23) here means man's ability to reason. Paul wishes the converts not to be turned aside from using their faculty of reasoning and the power of sane judgment. 'Quickly' does not mean here 'in a short while from now', but 'hastily'.

or excited: the tense is now present, indicating the sense of disquiet resulting and remaining from the initial shock. The same verb occurs in Mt. 24.6, also in connection with the false suggestion that the End is present whereas in fact only the signs of the End are to be seen. It is possible that Paul had the Matthean passage in mind.

either by spirit: Paul now mentions three possible sources of misunderstanding. 'Spirit' most naturally refers to the Holy Spirit but probably here signifies some utterance inspired by the Spirit, possibly (as distinct from 'word' following) an ecstatic utterance requiring interpretation (see on 1 Th. 5.19).

or by word: a general expression which could refer to a prophecy or sermon or any verbal communication.

or by letter purporting to be from us: 'purporting to be from us' must refer to 'letter', could also refer to 'word' and might even refer to all three media. Of these possibilities the last seems least likely to be correct because it is hard to think of an ecstatic utterance or revelation being communicated at a distance; it more naturally

Lord has come. ³ Let no one deceive you in any way; for that day will not come, unless the rebellion comes first, and the man of lawlessness is revealed, the son of perdition, ⁴ who opposes and exalts himself against every so-called god or object of worship, so that he takes his seat in the temple of God, proclaiming himself to

---

refers to some utterance from within the community. The same might be said of the second possibility (though cf. 2.15). The expression might well refer only to 'letter', for in 3.17 we find what appears to be a guard against the possibility of a spurious letter being mistaken for one from Paul and 1 Th. 5.27 (and possibly 2 Th. 3.14) may be an attempt to prevent misunderstanding or misuse of a letter. But whether Paul means a spurious letter or someone claiming to have a letter (without actually producing it) or a false interpretation of a letter (presumably 1 Thessalonians) is a matter of uncertainty; certainly the last of these could easily have happened.

the Day of the Lord has come: perfect tense to indicate an accomplished fact. Some scholars think that Paul had actually promised the Thessalonians that the Day would come within their lifetime (1 Th. 4.17 they interpret in this way); but even if he had said this (which we suggest is not the case) it would hardly have led to this notion that the Day had already come. It is more likely, if we are to think of 'by letter as from us' as a false reading of 1 Thessalonians, that the tension vividly expressed in such a sentence as 'Jesus . . . is delivering us from the End wrath' (1 Th. 1.10) had been dissolved in favour of a simple 'realized' eschatology (see the introduction to this section, above).

LAWLESSNESS NOW AND AT THE END 2.3-10

Paul's answer to the problem is to seek to restore the tension by emphasizing that events already taking place point to the nearness of the End, but that the final manifestation of the End is still to come and will be qualitatively different from the present ambiguous situation.

3. Let no one deceive you: the purpose of the instruction now to be given is to guard the converts against error, to 'comfort and establish them' (verse 17).

in any way: this refers back to the three possibilities spoken of in verse 2, but includes any and every other possibility as well.

for that day will not come: Greek has 'because unless the rebellion comes first'. RSV is perhaps slightly misleading, for the emphasis intended in the text seems to be not so much that certain events have still to take place and then the End will come, as that when the Day is here in its final manifest form it will be seen and known to be present because a number of extraordinary things will happen, first of which will be the unmasking of God's arch-enemy.

the rebellion comes first: here Paul uses imagery drawn probably from Dan.

11.36 (and cf. Isa. 14.13ff.; Ezek. 28.2). Rebellion, *apostasia*, could refer to political apostasy or military revolt in classical Greek, but in the LXX it denotes religious rebellion against God (cf. Jos. 22.22; Jer. 2.19). With the article (as here) it signifies a definite event of which the converts have knowledge (cf. verse 5). The thought is, we suggest, that when the moment comes for Christ to appear in glory and for all that rebels against God to be unmasked and cast out, the forces of evil will arise as never before in a last desperate effort against God. It is not the same thought as we find in Mk 13.6ff.; 1 Tim. 4.1ff.; 2 Tim. 3.1-9, where rebellion and lawlessness are 'signs of the End' (as here, too, in verses 4-7) for the final upsurge of evil here described is thought of as actually belonging to the complex of events which constitute the End.

the man of lawlessness is revealed: some MSS have 'man of sin', but 'man of lawlessness' is slightly better attested (the distinction in meaning is, in any case, not very great; cf. 1 Jn 3.4). It seems that Paul takes over some of the imagery of an Antichrist derived perhaps from certain Old Testament passages (cf. Isa. 14.13f.; Ezek. 28.2; Dan. 8.9f., 11.30ff.). This being is not Satan (in verse 9 he is distinguished from Satan), but he is the one in whom Satan's power is concentrated and in whom Satan is to be unmasked. The verb 'revealed' (*apokaluphthē*) points to the great *dénouement* when the Son of Man is revealed and at his revelation unmasks his enemies.

the son of perdition: a further description of Antichrist which points to his destiny. The construction is a Semitism and means 'he who is destined to be destroyed'. It is the lot of the enemies of Christ to suffer ruin (cf. 1 Th. 5.3; 2 Th. 1.8f.).

4. The point of verse 3 is that the End will see the unveiling of the forces of evil in a final paroxysm of rage just as it will display Christ in all his glory; that the former has not happened testifies that the latter also has not yet occurred. But this does not mean that Antichrist is not already at work, and verses 4-7 speak of this present activity of his which is itself a sign of the End and a pointer towards his future unmasking.

who opposes: cf. Dan. 7.25. In the New Testament this verb variously describes the opponents of Christ (Lk. 13.17) and the opponents of Paul (1 C. 16.9), and in 1 Tim. 5.14 seems to be used of Satan. The participle is intended to describe a present activity.

and exalts himself: almost certainly dependent on Dan. 11.36f. The verb is found in the New Testament only here and in 2 C. 12.7, where it means 'exalted above measure' (RSV 'too elated').

every so-called god or object of worship: the sense is that whatever men hold sacred, this is the stronghold against which evil sets and exalts itself.

so that he takes his seat in the Temple of God: the imagery appears to be drawn from Dan. 8.11-14, 12.11, where the reference is most likely to the desecration of the Temple in Jerusalem by Antiochus Epiphanes, who set up a heathen altar there in 168 B.C. Similar imagery is found in Mk 13.14. It is possible that Paul

be God. ⁵ Do you not remember that when I was still with you I told you this? ⁶And you know what is restraining him now so that he may be revealed in his time. ⁷ For the mystery of lawlessness is already at work; only he who now restrains it will do so until he is out of the way. ⁸And then the lawless one will be revealed, and the Lord Jesus will slay him with the breath of his mouth and destroy

---

alludes to Caligula's attempt, some ten years prior to this letter, to set up his shrine in the Temple, but it is equally possible that the allusion is a general one continuing with imagery ready to hand the idea of evil exalting itself against what men regard as sacred and attaching to itself the properties of divinity.

proclaiming himself to be god: the ultimate in evil is not simply to oppose what men hold sacred but to masquerade as divine. The verb 'proclaiming', *apodeiknumi*, can mean 'to designate', 'to set or shew forth' (RV), 'to claim' (NEB), or, as RSV, 'to proclaim'. The idea is similar to that in Mk 13.6, 21f.

5. In recalling to mind that he had often spoken of this (note the imperfect tense, meaning 'I used to tell' or 'I often spoke') Paul naturally turns to the first person singular. This is the only occurrence of this in the present letter, apart from the personal appendage in 3.17f.

6. The fact that Antichrist is already at work leads Paul to remind the converts that his power is strictly limited; at the unveiling at the Parousia, his power might be unleashed in a frenzied onslaught against his Judge, but in the meantime he enjoys only a freedom within bounds.

and you know: continues the sense of verse 5. Paul is not referring in verses 6–7 to some esoteric teaching but to something about which he has already told his converts.

what is restraining him now: 'now' could be a logical connection, 'and now you know' (RV and NEB), but is probably temporal, as RSV understands. 'Now' here corresponds to the 'now' (*arti*) in verse 7, and contrasts with 'then' in verse 8. Our difficulty is that Paul does not tell *us* here what is now restraining Antichrist's power and the matter is complicated by the use in this verse of the neuter ('that which restrains') and of the masculine in the next verse ('he who restrains'). Four different interpretations have been proposed:

(1) The historical interpretation, which sees in 'that which restrains' a reference to the Roman State and in 'he who now restrains' Claudius, the then reigning Emperor. Paul means, according to this interpretation, that once Claudius is gone the full force of Antichrist will be displayed under Nero. Advocates of this view remind us of the high evaluation placed by Paul upon the State and upon law and order in the service of God (cf. e.g. Rom. 13.1–7), but against the view it must be said that it assumes (quite unwarrantably) that Paul could already see that the 'poor fool' Claudius was qualitatively better than the then untried Nero.

(2) The legal interpretation, which sees in the Roman State the restraining thing and regards 'the restrainer' as any personification of this in any Emperor. The difficulty here is that the imagery describing Antichrist's activity (verse 4) referred in previous usage to the *abuse* of State power; are we to think that Paul now switches to acclaiming the State as the restrainer of Antichrist?

(3) The mythical interpretation, which takes the whole as a blend of history and mythology and thinks that no detail must be taken too literally. It refers to passages like Rev. 20 and similar themes in Jewish and Near-Eastern mythology. This description, on the other hand, does not read like the extravagant detail of Rev. 20 and similar apocalyptic writing. Furthermore, would Paul be able to say of such mythological themes, 'you know', as he does in this case?

(4) The gospel interpretation, which understands 'that which restrains' as gospel proclamation and 'he who restrains' as the preacher (some, though, we suggest, wrongly, understand 'Paul'). This seems to be most probably the meaning Paul intended. The present period prior to the End when the unmasking of Antichrist is withheld is a time when the gospel is preached and when men are given an opportunity to repent and believe. The insistence upon gospel proclamation is found in the Synoptics in just such a context (Mk 13.10 par.) and is the basic purpose for which the provision of an interval prior to the Parousia is granted (the same thought is expressed in 2 Pet. 3.8f.).

in his time: this does not mean when it suits Antichrist, but at the moment appointed by God (on 'time', *kairos*, see 1 Th. 2.17).

7. mystery of lawlessness: 'mystery' in the New Testament means something that can be understood only by revelation (and, in effect, only in terms of *the* revelation of God in Jesus Christ) (cf. Mk 4.11; Col. 1.26). Here 'mystery of lawlessness' contrasts with the revelation of the lawless one in verse 8. The present working of evil is properly understood by those who accept the gospel.

is already at work: the present activity of Antichrist is a prelude to the final paroxysm and therefore to the understanding a sign of the coming End. One might have expected Paul to write that 'lawlessness, though already (in the cross and resurrection) judged is *still* at work', but his standpoint here is the End itself from which standpoint present lawlessness must be seen as a foreshadowing of the End.

only he who now restrains it: see above on verse 6.

until he is out of the way: as we understand it, this will refer to the time when the opportunity for preaching, for repentance, and faith will cease and the End arrive. The same expression is found in Col. 2.14, in both cases the idea being the removal of an obstacle. It is only the provision of grace for preaching which stands in the way of the final unmasking of God's adversaries.

8. Having in verses 4-7 spoken of lawlessness as a sign of the End, Paul now turns again to the End itself (verses 8-10). The Parousia of Christ coincides with the unmasking of Antichrist (see verse 3 and the introduction to this section).

will slay: some MSS have here 'consume', a very similar word in Greek, which fits the imagery well but is probably not original. As 'Lord', Christ has already

him by his appearing and his coming. ⁹ The coming of the lawless one by the activity of Satan will be with all power and with pretended signs and wonders, ¹⁰ and with all wicked deception for those who are to perish, because they refused to love the truth and so be saved. ¹¹ Therefore God sends upon them a strong delusion,

---

triumphed over all antagonistic powers (cf. Mt. 28.18; Phil. 2.6ff.), but their final annihilation waits to the End (cf. also 1 C. 15.25f.; Heb. 10.13).

with the breath of his mouth: this is an allusion to Isa. 11.4 (cf. also Job 4.9; Wis. 11.20; Rev. 19.15, 21). The idea of a power proceeding from the person and presence of Christ is what Paul has in mind.

and destroy: the verb used here, *katargeō*, means to render inactive and so to abolish. It is the same word which Paul uses in 1 C. 15.26 of the final abolition of death 'the last enemy' (in 2 Tim. 1.10 death is said to be abolished already, this same verb being used).

by his appearing and his coming: the two expressions in this verse are parallel, 'will slay with the breath of his mouth' being more or less repeated in 'destroy by his appearing and his coming'. On 'appearing' and 'coming' see 1 Th. 2.19. The two words, though referring to the same event here, are not exactly synonyms, the former carrying the idea of splendour (it was the word used in secular Greek of the display of a divinity), the latter meaning simply 'presence'; NEB renders together 'the radiance of his coming' (cf. the similar expression in 2 Tim. 4.1, 'his appearing and his kingdom').

9. Mention of the powerful presence in glory of Jesus leads Paul on to a brief description of the 'parousia' of the lawless one. He makes three points about this: the power behind it is Satan's (verse 9*a*), the power attendant is displayed in signs and wonders (verse 9*b*), and the power it has over the spectators results in the seduction of the (attendant) wicked (verse 10).

by the activity of Satan: RSV rightly distinguishes between the word here rendered 'activity' (*energein*; also in verse 11) which means power in action (cf. RV 'working'), and the word in the next phrase 'power' (*dunamis*) meaning power as such. According to the imagery used by Paul, the man of lawlessness is not Satan but embodies in himself Satan's powers and character.

with all power and with pretended signs and wonders: 'All' could refer to the three substantives that follow or only to the first; similarly 'pretended' could refer only to the last or to all three. Probably the sense is that the Parousia of the lawless one will be attended with all the trappings of power expressed both in pretended signs and pretended wonders (RSV is, we suggest, better than RV; and NEB seems unwise in treating 'power' as an adjective or in counting 'lie' which lacks the article in Greek as 'the Lie'). A parallel expression is used of Christ's miracles in Ac. 2.22, 'mighty works and wonders and signs', which showed him to be 'approved by God'. The signs and wonders of the lawless one contrast with these miracles, having the character of lies. As signs they point to deceit and as wonders or spectacles they have the effect of deceiving the beholders (verse 10). 'Pretended' translates the Greek word for 'lie' or 'falsehood', the opposite of what is true; it does not mean 'pretended' in the sense of 'imagined'.

10. The description of Antichrist's attendant wonders leads on to the third point, that his appearing will dazzle and seduce his own followers.

with all wicked deception: lit. 'all deceit of wickedness', the construction being as in the phrase before which was lit. 'signs and wonders of falsehood'. The deception proceeds from wickedness (*adikia* is, for Paul, the opposite of 'righteousness', cf. Rom. 3.5, 6.13).

for those who are to perish: the Greek has a present participle possibly because Paul is describing the future event as though it were happening or, more probably, because he thinks of the destruction of the wicked as a process already begun (as in 1 C. 1.18 also: cf. the same for those being saved, 1 Th. 1.10). Paul thinks of Antichrist's attendant host, the ones who are perishing, being dazzled by his appearing just as the 'saints' will 'marvel at' the appearance of Christ (1.10).

because they refused to love the truth: lit. 'they did not welcome the love of the truth'. The saints marvel at Christ at his Parousia because of a prior response to the gospel; likewise those dazzled by the wonders of Antichrist's appearing are those who have already rejected the gospel (cf. 1.8) and by their rejection already laid claim to be amongst Antichrist's attendant train. The expression 'the love of the truth' appears nowhere else in the New Testament or in the LXX. 'Truth' is not the quality of truthfulness so much as the objective 'truth of God' (cf. Rom. 1.25) and the expression is another way of describing 'those who do not know God ... who do not obey the gospel of our Lord Jesus' (1.8). On 'love' see 1 Th. 1.3.

THE MYSTERY OF UNBELIEF 2.11–12

Paul has raised the matter of unbelief and the problem why some believe and others do not, why some lay claim to be amongst Christ's worshippers at the Parousia and others lay claim to be in Antichrist's train. Near to hand lay the answer that some are drawn of God to faith in Christ, others are attracted by Satan to allegiance to Antichrist; but to the mind schooled in the Old Testament and committed to the gospel of Jesus Christ—both certain of the sovereignty of God—this would admit of an intolerable dualism and could not for a moment be contemplated. Therefore, whilst in verses 13f. God is shown to be responsible for the whole process of salvation, he is also, in verses 11f., not excluded from activity in the process of unbelief leading to condemnation.

11. Therefore God sends: the Greek *dia touto* means 'to this end', as in Rom. 1.26, 28. Having refused to love the truth, God furthers their destiny (cf. Rom. 1.24ff.). Unbelief is not some activity entirely independent of God, nor is the result seen by Paul as a triumph for evil, but a just decision of God. It is in accord with the Old Testament that the New Testament refuses to accord evil and unbelief any

to make them believe what is false, ¹² so that all may be condemned
who did not believe the truth but had pleasure in unrighteousness.

13 But we are bound to give thanks to God always for you,
brethren beloved by the Lord, because God chose you from the
beginning to be saved, through sanctification by the Spirit and belief

---

independence over against God (cf. Exod. 4.21; 1 Kg. 22.23; Ezek. 14.9; Mk 4.11f.;
Rom. 9.18).

a strong delusion: lit. with RV 'a working of error'.

to make them believe what is false: this is the first step in a two-fold purpose
(the second, final result comes in verse 12). Those who reject the objective truth of
God embrace what is false (Greek has 'the lie', cf. Rom. 1.25) and succumb to the
deceit practised by Satan, and this happens somehow in accord with the intentions
of God.

12. so that all may be condemned: this is the second and ultimate purpose of
the 'strong delusion' sent upon the unbeliever. The thought reverts to the scene at
the End when those who through their unbelief have laid claim to the verdict of
condemnation receive their reward. The tense of the verb is aorist, indicating a
single event. With the slaying of the lawless one goes the condemnation and
exclusion of his train. For 'judge' (*krinō*) in the sense of 'condemn' cf. e.g. Rom.
2.12; Jas 5.9; Rev. 18.8.

who did not believe the truth: to love the truth means to believe the truth,
which means to 'obey the gospel' (1.8). Paul is speaking of those who have
disobeyed the gospel, disbelieved the truth. The construction here (the verb
followed by the dative) is unusual in Paul (it is found only here other than in
quotations) and suggests not so much putting one's trust in something as giving
credence to something; far from trusting in God's truth, the unbeliever does not
even accord it credence.

pleasure in unrighteousness: 'unrighteousness' renders the same Greek word
which in verse 10 is translated 'wicked'. The wicked deception practiced by the
lawless one finds a reception in the unbeliever which the gospel and truth did not.
'Have pleasure' translates the same verb (*eudokeō*) as is found in 1 Th. 2.8 and 3.1.
It signifies a positive approval (cf. NEB 'their deliberate choice') and a sense of
contentment with the approved object or person. It is the same word that expresses
God's glad approval of his Son at his baptism (Mt. 3.17).

THE MYSTERY OF FAITH 2.13-15

Verses 13-15 examine the same matter as verses 11-12, only now (and with
thankfulness) from the standpoint of those who believe. It is the other half of
the same mystery with which Paul is here concerned. In this brief rationale of

faith there are three sections: first the election of God, the divine intention that the converts should be saved (verse 13); secondly, the historical occurrence through which this call was actualized and effected (verse 14); and thirdly, the lesson to be drawn from this, namely to persevere in faith and obedience (verse 15).

13. But we are bound to give thanks: word for word, though with a slight and insignificant change of order, as in 1.3 (which see). Clearly this introduction marks a new section, but a section closely connected with the thought of verses 11–12. The contrast of sin and grace which Paul draws in Rom. 5.12–21 shows that parallelism has its limits! Similarly here, unbelief and belief are contrasted, but with an inevitable disproportion. Unbelief is to be noted, understood, and even reckoned with as somehow involved in the purposes of God; but faith is something for which Paul feels bound to give continual thanks.

beloved by the Lord: in 1 Th. 1.4 the converts are 'beloved by God', also in the context of God's election, as here. The expression is found in Dt. 33.12 where, of course, 'Lord' means God. Here, however, 'Lord' probably means Jesus, for otherwise 'God' in the next clause would be superfluous and because 'beloved by Jesus' is particularly apt in the context where Antichrist's attendant followers are being contrasted with Christ's followers.

because God chose you: the verb used here is found only three times in the New Testament; in Phil. 1.22 and Heb. 11.25 it means 'choose' in the sense of 'prefer'. It is not Paul's usual way of referring to God's election but he is probably influenced by the contrast being drawn in this passage. Over against those who refuse to love the truth and to whom God sends a strong delusion, the converts are 'preferred' (cf. the same verb in the LXX of Dt. 26.18).

from the beginning: some MSS read 'God has chosen you a first-fruit' (*aparchēn* for *ap' archēs*), an expression which Paul uses both of Christ (1 C. 15.23) and of Christians (Rom. 16.5; 1 C. 16.15). Some commentators accept this, but the attestation for 'from the beginning' is slightly better and the sense, in the context, is also preferable. The Greek *archē* means 'first' and can be used meaning first in rank or order and so could mean 'sovereignty' or 'authority'. It could also have a local sense and is used, for example, in Ac. 10.11 of the corners of a sheet. But its regular sense in the New Testament is temporal, sometimes meaning the beginning of the world (Mk 10.6; 2 Pet. 3.4, etc.), sometimes the beginning of Jesus' ministry (Lk. 1.2; Jn 15.27), and sometimes the beginning of Christian faith (1 Jn 1.24; 2 Jn 5). The suggestion has been made that Paul here means the commencement of his preaching ministry in Thessalonica (cf. Phil. 4.15), but in the absence of any qualifying phrase such as 'our gospel' (as in Phil. 4.15) and bearing in mind the context here, it is best to interpret the meaning as 'from the beginning of the world', a thought similar to Eph. 1.4 (and cf. 1 C. 2.7; Col. 1.26). NEB 'from the beginning of time' shares this view.

to be saved: the purpose of God's calling is salvation (on which see 1 Th. 5.8). Probably Paul's mind looks towards the ultimate end of salvation, 'the glory of our

in the truth. 14 To this he called you through our gospel, so that you may obtain the glory of our Lord Jesus Christ. 15 So then, brethren, stand firm and hold to the traditions which you were taught by us, either by word of mouth or by letter.

16 Now may our Lord Jesus Christ himself, and God our Father, who loved us and gave us eternal comfort and good hope through

---

Lord Jesus Christ' which the believer is to obtain (verse 14) but he leaves this for the moment and expands first the idea of salvation in terms of the process leading up to that goal. This process is two-fold:

through sanctification by the Spirit: the same expression is found in 1 Pet. 1.2. As 1 Th. 4.3–8 explained, sanctification is part of God's will and is made possible by the Spirit (4.8). It is the work of the Spirit so to purify the converts as to ensure that they are presentable at the Parousia of Christ (1 Th. 3.13, 5.23).

and belief in the truth: ethical reform is only half of the process of salvation, the other half being faith in the gospel by which claim is already laid upon the goal of salvation. Sanctification by the Spirit does not overlook human effort (cf. Phil. 2.12f.), nor is belief in the truth possible apart from the Spirit who authenticates the gospel (cf. 1 Th. 1.5), so it would be dangerous to suggest (as some scholars do) that these expressions point on the one hand to the Godward and on the other hand to the manward aspects of salvation. 'Truth' is here the truth of God revealed in Christ and so is the equivalent of the gospel, the expression being due, perhaps, to the comparison with the deceived of verse 10 who 'refused to love the truth'. It is both the message in which faith reposes and the power which calls forth and makes the response of faith possible (the genitive is both subjective and objective in this context).

14. To this: God's purpose of salvation is effected in an historical event, the response of faith to the gospel proclaimed. Therefore 'to this' signifies the entire purpose of God (salvation, sanctification, and faith) and does not simply mean 'faith', nor 'sanctification and faith' (both of which are grammatically possible).

he called you through our gospel: the process is very similar to that described in Rom. 8.30. Previous purpose leads to the act in time of calling, which leads to ultimate glory. Here the stage of justification (cf. in Rom. 8.30 'those whom he called he also justified') is omitted, probably because it is presupposed in the term 'gospel' here, the news of God's decision to account righteous those who believe in Jesus Christ. On 'our gospel' see 1 Th. 1.5. God's election is worked out in time through preaching which can therefore also be regarded as God's call.

so that you may obtain the glory: as in Rom. 8.30 'those whom he justified he also glorified'. The consummation of faith and sanctification is the participation in Christ's glory at the End. Here, the ambiguity found in 1.10 is no longer present; the thought is that the believer 'obtains' (the same word as in 1 Th. 5.9 used of 'salvation') similar glory to that belonging to Christ (cf. Rom. 8.17; 1 Jn 3.2).

15. So then: neither sanctification nor faith are altogether the work of man, but neither are they altogether the work of God excusing man from active, serious, and persistent co-operation. Therefore Paul can turn directly, as he does here, from the account of God's fore-ordination of salvation, sanctification, and faith, to an exhortation to the converts to stand firm. It is because of God's election and calling that such an exhortation is meaningful.

stand firm: see on 1 Th. 3.8.

hold to the traditions: this is probably not a second requirement, but the same thing as 'stand firm' put another way. To stand firm is to hold fast to the gospel message (the same combination of ideas is found in 1 C. 11.2, 15.1). 'Traditions' (*paradoseis*) belongs, like 'deliver' (*paradidōmi*), 'receive' (*paralambanō*), and 'teach' (*didaskō*), to the early church's vocabulary relating to the transmission of the gospel message, the imparting of its ethical and doctrinal consequences, and to the acceptance of these. This 'tradition' terminology will have been adopted into the Christian vocabulary from Jewish custom and usage, for the Jews were used to thinking of their law as 'delivered' by God to Moses who in turn 'delivered' it to Joshua, and so on, and also were accustomed to speaking of the 'traditions of the fathers' (cf. Mt. 15.2). There is no need to search amongst the language of the mystery religions of the time (as some have done) to discover a possible origin of such terms in the Christian churches. In this verse 'traditions' probably includes not only ethical rules of behaviour (in this sense of the word cf. Rom. 6.17; 1 C. 11.2) but the gospel message itself also (in this sense cf. 1 C. 15.3f.).

which you were taught by us: it is possible that Paul means 'stand firm, in the gospel' and 'hold fast to the moral instruction we taught you', but more probably by 'which we taught you' he refers to his entire ministry of preaching, teaching, and exhortation.

either by word of mouth: most naturally this refers to the ministry of Paul and his companions at Thessalonica, but it could also include any messages sent by the apostles (as Timothy was sent, according to 1 Th. 3.2, to establish the converts in the faith and to exhort them).

or by letter: most naturally refers to 1 Thessalonians.

PRAYER 2.16–17

Before moving on to a final section dealing with matters of behaviour, Paul closes this section with a prayer. The similarity with 1 Th. 3.11ff. is marked.

16. Now may our Lord Jesus Christ himself: unlike 1 Th. 3.11, Christ is mentioned first in this invocation, but it seems unlikely that there is any special significance in this.

who loved us: Paul speaks variously of the love of God (2 Th. 3.5; Rom. 5.5) and of the love of Christ (Rom. 8.35; 2 C. 5.14). Here the participle is singular and could refer to 'God our Father' only, but most probably refers to Father and Son. In 1 Th. 3.11 the Father and Son are so closely united as to allow their action to be covered by a singular verb. The aorist tense probably indicates that Paul is thinking

grace,[17] comfort your hearts and establish them in every good work and word.

3 Finally, brethren, pray for us, that the word of the Lord may speed on and triumph, as it did among you, [2] and that we may be delivered from wicked and evil men; for not all have faith. [3] But the Lord is faithful; he will strengthen you and guard you from

---

of the event in which this love was supremely displayed, the crucifixion of Christ (cf. Gal. 2.20 'who loved me and gave himself for me', and cf. Jn 3.16; 1 Jn 4.10).

eternal comfort: 'comfort' translates the noun, *paraklēsis*, from the same root as the verb, *parakaleō*, found in 1 Th. 2.11 and 3.2 and there translated 'exhort'; perhaps 'encouragement' (as in NEB) captures more the ideas in the Greek word of gentle consolation and firm summons. Paul is thinking here of the cross and resurrection as the display of God's love and an eternal summons and encouragement to faith and hope. 'Eternal' thus means not only temporally unbounded but sharing in the character of God's existence (see on 2 Th. 1.9) for the comfort in question is bound up with his own person and character.

and good hope: the cross and resurrection not only call man to his senses but stretch out to him 'good', i.e. beneficial and sound, hope. (On 'hope', characteristic of the Christian, see 1 Th. 1.3.)

through grace: an adverbial expression indicating the source of the love, comfort, and hope spoken of; all stem from God's grace (on which, see 1 Th. 1.1).

17. comfort your hearts: this verb describes something that human beings can do (in Col. 4.8 and Eph. 6.22 Tychicus is sent 'to comfort your hearts'), but it is also something for which it is necessary to pray. On 'comfort' see verse 16, and on 'heart' see 1 Th. 2.4.

and establish them: this is the same petition as in 1 Th. 3.13, that God will direct the course of the converts' faith and sanctification with a view to their being 'unblamable in holiness . . . at the coming of our Lord Jesus' (1 Th. 3.13).

in every good work and word: the sanctification for which Paul prays is comprehensive, involving all that the converts do and say.

INSTRUCTION IN CHRISTIAN FAITH AND LIFE 3.1–15

As in the first letter (cf. 4.1ff.) the apostle, having dealt with doctrinal problems, turns now to matters of Christian behaviour and in this chapter is concerned especially with the problem of idleness (verses 6–15). But first he desires of his converts that they should pray for the missionaries and their work (verses 1–2) and speaks to them of the faithfulness of God in completing in the converts that which he has already begun (verses 3–5).

REQUEST FOR PRAYER 3.1–2

1. Finally, brethren: see on 1 Th. 4.1.

pray for us: as in 1 Th. 5.23ff., Paul here follows his own prayer for the converts with a request for their prayers. Here, however, the request is for a particular object, whereas in the first letter it was undefined. The tense of the verb is present which probably carries the nuance, 'keep on praying as you are doing', and certainly implies continuous action. The word order of the Greek 'pray, brethren, for us' makes the request quite emphatic.

that the word of the Lord: this is the first of two objectives towards which the converts' prayers are asked to be directed (the second comes in verse 2). On 'word of the Lord' see 1 Th. 2.8. The request for prayer recognizes the participation of all Christians in the church's mission and that it is not the prerogative or responsibility only of those who preach or teach.

may speed on: the verb used here, *trechō*, is the usual one for 'running' (cf. e.g. Mt. 7.28; 28.8) and is used a number of times in the New Testament of the Christian progress in faith and life (cf. e.g. 1 C. 9.26; Gal. 5.7; Heb. 12.1) but is found only here in the New Testament with reference to the spread of the gospel message. The image is found in Ps. 147.15 which may have been in Paul's mind in writing. There is, in the imagery, a sense of urgency characteristic of the way in which the church's mission is regarded in the New Testament.

and triumph: the Greek verb is 'be glorified' (cf. on 1.10). Possibly the imagery continues from the previous expression and the idea is that the gospel may so speed on in its race as to achieve its goal, the winner's crown of triumph (this means taking the verb which is passive in form in an active sense: notice that similar imagery is applied to the Christian in 1 C. 9.24f.). But it is probable that the imagery of running a race is dropped in the second verb and that the thought is simply that the gospel message might be gladly received (which gives to the verb its passive meaning and is akin to the idea of Ac. 13.48 which speaks of Gentiles who 'were glad and glorified the word of God'). Either interpretation seems more likely to be correct than that which understands 'be glorified' of miracles attaching to preaching (though the thought of preaching *is* closely allied to that of healing and miracle working in e.g. Ac. 4.29f.; Rom. 15.19).

as it did among you: lit. 'as also with you'. RSV (and NEB) understand this as a reference to the mission and its success at Thessalonica; but Paul may be thinking of the continued welcome given by the converts to the gospel, and quite possibly both past and present might be in mind, Paul meaning 'that the word may speed on and be glorified as it was and is with you'.

2. and that we may be delivered: this is the second objective of the converts' prayers. It was an established fact that the gospel could not be heard without the ministry of a preacher (Rom. 1.14), so the prayer for the gospel to speed on leads naturally to the prayer that Paul and his companions may be delivered from those who would hinder their work. On 'deliver' which carries the sense of snatching from danger (hence NEB 'rescue') see 1 Th. 1.10.

evil. ⁴And we have confidence in the Lord about you, that you are doing and will do the things which we command. ⁵ May the Lord direct your hearts to the love of God and to the steadfastness of Christ.

---

from wicked and evil men: in 1 Th. 2.16 Paul spoke of the Jews who, amongst other faults, hindered the progress of the gospel. In view of the definite article here ('*the* wicked and evil men') in the Greek, and the aorist tense of the verb 'deliver' it is right to think of a definite situation and a particular group of people, rather than of opponents and opposition in general. Here Paul refers to the Jews at Corinth who, according to Ac. 18.6, 'opposed and reviled' him as he preached to them and who later 'made a united attack upon Paul and brought him before the tribunal'. 'Wicked', *atopos*, means basically 'not in place' and so comes to mean 'strange' or 'absurd' and it is in this sense that RV ('unreasonable') and NEB ('wrong-headed') understand it. But in later Greek this word came to mean out of place in the sense of 'monstrous', 'disgusting', and this is its sense in the LXX and in other New Testament occurrences (Lk. 23.41; Ac. 25.5, where it means something like 'deserving of punishment' and Ac. 28.6, where it means 'calamitous'). It is therefore probable that RSV 'wicked' is what Paul intended. On 'evil', *ponēros*, see on 1 Th. 5.22.

for not all have faith: lit. 'for not of all men (is) the faith', which could mean that not all men exercise faith, or that not all belong to 'the Faith'. The difference is, in any case, not very great. It might seem that Paul is here expressing a platitude, for it is obvious that the enemies of the gospel are not themselves Christians; actually, he is giving the reason behind the activity of evil men in opposing the gospel. Faith is, for Paul, the great divide, the means by which one lays claim already to the eschatological events, to the verdict of acquittal, and to the blessings of 'the age to come'; lack of faith is the means by which one lays claim, on the other hand, to be excluded at that Day, and to share the character of the present 'evil age', to follow 'the evil One'.

The Faithfulness of God 3.3-5

The formal reason for the introduction of this theme is the mention of the lack of faith of some men in verse 2; to this contrasts the faithfulness of God (the play on *pistis*, faith, and *pistos*, faithful, is similar to that in Rom. 3.3). The real reason for this theme is the mention of opposition to the gospel which reminds Paul that not only is he suffering affliction in Corinth but his converts in Thessalonica are also a persecuted community (1.4; cf. 1 Th. 1.6, 2.14). They are to take heart and strength from the assurance that God is faithful. The apostle reverts to the thought of 2.13-15, as though the prayer and prayer request of 2.16-3.2 were a parenthesis.

3. But the Lord is faithful: elsewhere Paul speaks of the faithfulness of 'God'

(1 C. 1.9, 10.13; 2 C. 1.18, and the unexpressed subject of 1 Th. 5.24), but 'Lord' here will mean Jesus, continuing the emphasis on Christ in contrast and opposition to Antichrist, which features so much in this letter. 'Faithful', *pistos*, can mean 'believing' (as in Jn 20.27; 1 Tim. 6.2); but generally in the New Testament it means 'credible' or 'worthy of belief and trust', and this is always its meaning when applied to God. NEB is right in translating 'the Lord is to be trusted'.

he will strengthen you: the same verb is used in 1 Th. 3.2 where Paul speaks of Timothy 'establishing' the converts in their faith. Although this can be seen therefore as a human activity, it is fundamentally God's work, and it is because of this that Paul has confidence concerning the converts ('he who calls is faithful, and he will do it', 1 Th. 5.24).

and guard you from evil: Paul has already said enough to show that this does not mean that God will enable the converts to escape persecution and affliction (cf. 1 Th. 3.3; 2 Th. 1.4f.), but rather that God can be relied upon to sustain their faith through the difficulties of affliction so that evil will not triumph over them. The word 'evil' (on which see 1 Th. 5.22) might have a quite general reference if we take the word as being neuter—'the evil thing', i.e. any evil thing; but it may well be intended as masculine and a reference to 'the evil one', i.e. the devil (as in RV and NEB). This certainly seems to be the meaning in Mt. 13.19; Eph. 6.16; 1 Jn 2.13, 3.12, 5.18, and might well be the meaning also in Mt. 6.13. Such an interpretation would suit the context here well, for in verse 2 we read of 'evil men' and in chapter 2 learn of 'the lawless one', Antichrist, and his minions. If this is the right interpretation, Paul may well have in mind not only the present assaults of the devil in affliction and persecution ('temptations' through which the faithful God guards his people, cf. 1 C. 10.13), but also the final manifestation of the evil one at the End (cf. 2.3ff.), of which the present troubles are a foretaste and prelude (just as the final petition of the Lord's prayer, Mt. 6.13, may well have the same double significance).

4. And we have confidence in the Lord: the verb here is in the perfect tense, indicating an enduring confidence. Paul's assurance concerns the converts but is not grounded in them; it is grounded in the trustworthiness of God.

the things which we command: this verb is from the same root as the noun 'instructions' in 1 Th. 4.2. Probably Paul means his instructions in a very broad sense, involving his original teaching during the mission at Thessalonica, his teaching in the first letter, what he has already said in this letter, and the instructions which follow (cf. 'we command', again in verse 6).

5. The movement of thought noticeable in 2.14-16 from confidence in God concerning the converts, through concern about their response to God's call, to prayer for them to remain faithful, is found here in the movement from confidence 'in the Lord' (verse 3), through assurance as to their response (verse 4) to prayer for the converts (verse 5).

May the Lord direct your hearts: as throughout this section, 'Lord' will mean Jesus. The verb is that used in 1 Th. 3.11 (which see). The expression 'direct the

6 Now we command you, brethren, in the name of our Lord Jesus Christ, that you keep away from any brother who is living in idleness and not in accord with the tradition that you received from

---

heart' is found in the LXX (e.g. 1 Chr. 29.18; 2 Chr. 12.14, 19.3, 20.33; etc.) where it signifies a dedication of the whole personality towards the attainment of some goal. Here the meaning is not so much that God will guide the Thessalonians (cf. 'guide our way' in 1 Th. 3.11) as that he will keep the converts firmly set upon their path towards the attainment of the two goals, love of God and the steadfastness of Christ; it concerns the integrity of the 'inner man' rather than the propitiousness of outward circumstances.

to the love of God: as in Rom. 5.5, the genitive could be understood objectively 'the love God has for us' (so NEB and Moffatt) or subjectively 'our love towards God'. But in Rom. 5.5 it is very probable (in view of verses 6–8) that it is God's love for us which is intended and in Rom. 8.39 and 2 C. 13.13 this is certainly the case. Possibly here both aspects are present in Paul's thought: it is towards an apprehension of God's love that the 'inner man' controlling actions, words, and thoughts is to be directed, and apprehension of this love will induce a corresponding love for God in response.

and to the steadfastness of Christ: again the genitive is a problem. The expression might mean 'the patience displayed by Christ' (as Moffatt understands with 'towards Christ's patience'), taking the genitive subjectively; or, taking it objectively, 'our patience as we wait for Christ to return in glory'. But again, it is possible that Paul intended something of both ideas; 'may the converts be dedicated towards an apprehension of Christ's patience such as will instil in them patient waiting for the End' is probably the meaning. On 'patience', see 1 Th. 1.3.

AGAINST IDLENESS 3.6–15

Evidently the idlers of 1 Th. 5.14 (cf. 4.11f.) had not responded to Paul's exhortation or to the admonition of the congregation, for Paul has a report that there are still some who are idle busybodies (verse 11). Many commentators, remarking on the length with which Paul treats his matter, assume that it had become a large-scale problem. However, length of discussion does not necessarily indicate the size of the problem, and may well rather be a pointer to Paul's serious pastoral concern for his converts. Besides, the discussion is not particularly protracted or repetitive (which one might expect in a 'crisis' situation) but runs quickly through the basic principles involved. Thus, he says; keep away from idlers (verse 6) and rather imitate our example (verse 7) of working for our keep (verse 8)—thereby setting you a pattern (verse 9); we also gave explicit command (verse 10) which some apparently disobey (verse 11); these we admonish (verse 12) and all of you we encourage (verse 13); further disobedience now must lead to brotherly discipline (verses 14–15). The need for this discussion of the whole matter over against the short injunctions in the first letter is not necessarily because the problem had grown worse but because the offenders persisted in their misbehaviour. The glowing praise of 2.3f. and 3.4 tells against any suggestion of a crisis in the church.

Another question which is raised by this section is whether the idlers were the ones who, having dissolved the eschatological tension of the present time held to a 'realized eschatology' and sought to anticipate the conditions of the End time (the sort of people who, according to 2.2, were suggesting that 'the day of the Lord has come'). Whilst it is possible that the idlers were those who held to a 'realized eschatology', it remains also possible that the idleness arose from a false understanding of the mutual responsibilities of Christian 'brothers' (as suggested in 1 Th. 4.11), and that some supposed it was open to them to exploit the generous care of their 'brethren' towards them. The discussion of verses 6–15 certainly seems to answer an ethical problem of this nature rather than a problem of 'realized eschatology'.

6. Now we command you, brethren: introducing a new section (cf. 1 Th. 4.1, 10, 5.12, 14). 'Command' here has a military ring about it; it is used in classical Greek of a general giving orders to his troops, and in the New Testament it is the verb used of Jesus giving his disciples their marching orders (Mt. 10.5), of Jesus disposing in ranks the thousands whom he fed (Mk 8.6), and of his command to the unclean spirit of the man, Legion (Lk. 8.29), though it is also used often enough in a milder sense of 'tell' or 'instruct'.

in the name of the Lord Jesus Christ: this is not a simple invocation; the solemnity and authority of Paul's command is given its proper basis by reference to Paul's own authority as apostle of Christ. It is with the delegated authority of Christ himself that he speaks to the converts (cf. on 1 Th. 2.13). There is no inconsistency in, at the same time, referring to the converts as 'brethren', nor is this term intended to soften the seriousness of his command; it is precisely because they are 'brethren' that he can command them in Christ's name (cf. his words in 3.15). A similar authoritative expression was used by Paul, according to Ac. 16.18, in exorcizing a spirit.

that you keep away from: this verb, *stellō*, is found only here and in 2 C. 8.20 in the New Testament (though a compound verb similar in form and meaning is also found some four times). Originally it means 'to get ready', 'to equip', especially referring to equipping an army for an expedition or a ship for sailing. Then it comes to mean 'to bring together' or 'gather up'—as, for instance, one gathers or tucks up clothes; and from this comes the sense of an inner gathering up or withdrawal, and so of 'flinching' and 'avoiding'. This is the sense here. Withdrawal from brethren who are 'out of step' was part of the early church's machinery of discipline.

Within the New Testament we find besides this instance similar disciplinary measures described in Mt. 18.15–18; 1 C. 5.1–13; 1 Tim. 1.20, and Tit. 3.10. Excommunication according to a graded system was practised in Judaism (cf.

us. **7** For you yourselves know how you ought to imitate us; we were not idle when we were with you, **8** we did not eat any one's bread without paying, but with toil and labour we worked night and day, that we might not burden any of you. **9** It was not because we have not that right, but to give you in our conduct an example to imitate. **10** For even when we were with you, we gave you this command: If any one will not work, let him not eat. **11** For we

---

Jn 9.22, 12.42, 16.2) and was also familiar in the Qumrân community (cf. e.g. 1QS. 8.21ff.).

any brother: the command is far from encouraging a form of world escape for Paul speaks not of shunning contact with non-Christians but of a disciplinary avoidance of fellow-Christians ('brother' in this sense) who are unwilling to conform to Christian standards.

who is living in idleness: lit. 'who walks *ataktōs*', the adverb cognate with 'the idle' of 1 Th. 5.14 (which see). Clearly the expression means more than simply anyone unemployed; 'to walk' signifies a comportment and attitude, and *ataktōs* implies more than lack of work. The whole expression indicates people whose custom and pleasure it is to loiter, laze, and exploit the hard work of others (cf. NEB 'who fall into idle habits'). They are in this respect unruly, unwilling to exert themselves, and unwilling to conform to the standards incumbent upon members of the Christian congregation.

and not in accord with the tradition that you received: cf. on 'tradition' 2.15. As in that verse, Paul may here be referring to his entire ministry ('tradition that you received' is a general expression) rather than to moral teaching in particular, though the latter fits the context here and is, perhaps, suggested by verse 10. On 'received', see on 1 Th. 2.13. RSV (with NEB, RV margin, and Moffatt) accepts the MSS which read 'you received', *parelabete*; but some MSS read 'they received', *parelabon* (and the irregular form *parelabosan*), which is accepted by RV, whilst AV follows yet other MSS which read 'he received', *parelabe*. The last is poorly attested, but the other two readings are fairly evenly attested. The context perhaps favours 'they received', expanding the idea of living in idleness and affirming that they know it to be wrong. Furthermore verse 7 begins with 'for you yourselves know', marking, perhaps, an emphatic contrast with 'they received'. A scribal error of this sort could easily arise; 'you know' in verse 7, ending in *ete* could have caught the scribe's eye as he copied 'received' in this verse so that he wrote 'you received' (ending in *ete*) instead of 'they received'. On balance there seems more in favour of RV 'they', but the general meaning of the verse is not affected.

7. Verses 7–10 explicate 'the tradition you received from us' of verse 6 in terms of Paul's example and express command.

For you yourselves know: see on 1 Th. 2.1. The failure of some to live according to the tradition is due not to ignorance but to unwillingness.

how you ought: the Greek verb 'it is necessary', *dei*, probably carries here a sense of divine compulsion meaning rather than 'it is ethically right' or 'it is propitious', something like 'it is in accord with the divine purpose for you . . .' (cf. 2.13f.).

to imitate us: see on 1 Th. 1.6. The sense really is both 'you know that you ought to imitate us' and 'you know in what manner you ought to imitate us' (Moffatt, in his translation, allows only this latter sense). The example Paul set his converts is now expanded, first with two negative statements (verses 7*b* and 8*a*) and then positively (verses 8*b*ff.).

we were not idle: a reference to the orderly and responsible behaviour of the missionaries whilst at Thessalonica, which included willingness to work hard for their upkeep. Paul uses the verb from the same root as 'idleness' in verse 6; it is the only occurrence of this verb in the New Testament.

8. **we did not eat anyone's bread without paying:** not being 'loafers' (Rutherford's and Moffatt's expression), the missionaries were able to pay for their keep and not be an expense to others. The expression 'to eat bread' is a Semitism referring not simply to having a meal (Moffatt gives this impression with 'we did not take free meals'), but to gaining one's livelihood (cf. e.g. Gen. 3.19; 2 Sam. 9.7). Paul means that his whole board and lodging was not an expense to someone else but something for which he paid. 'Without paying' translates a Greek adverb, *dōrean*, which in the New Testament means variously 'freely' (Rom. 3.24), 'without cause' (Jn 15.25), 'in vain' (Gal. 2.21), and, as here, 'without paying', the exact sense being determined by the context.

but with toil and labour: the example given by Paul is now described positively. On this part of the verse, cf. 1 Th. 2.9. Although these two passages are similar, in the first Paul refers to his manual work in defence of his motives in preaching the gospel (i.e. he did not preach to make money), whereas here he calls to mind his work as an example to those who prefer to be idle.

9. **not because we have not that right:** the example has added force when it is realized that as accredited preachers of the gospel Paul and his companions had the right to be supported by the converts in recognition of their work (see on 1 Th. 2.6). 'Right' translates a Greek word, *exousia*, meaning 'freedom to do something' and so 'power' and 'authority', as here.

that we might give you in our conduct: lit. 'that we might give you ourselves an example'. By this, Paul indicates that the whole comportment of the missionaries, the waiving of their rights, their industry and responsibility, was a living example for the converts to follow. On 'example' see on 1 Th. 1.7.

10. From example, Paul now turns to command; the tradition familiar to the converts was not only expressed in the missionaries' behaviour but was also made explicit in their teaching.

we gave you this commandment: lit. 'we commanded you this', the same verb being used here as in verses 4 and 6 (which see). The tense here is imperfect, sug-

hear that some of you are living in idleness, mere busybodies, not doing any work. ¹² Now such persons we command and exhort in the Lord Jesus Christ to do their work in quietness and to earn their own living. ¹³ Brethren, do not be weary in well-doing.

---

gesting a continued or repeated action, hence Moffatt translates 'we used to charge you'. Part of the 'traditions' taught to the converts was this rule of life.

if any one will not work: the emphasis is upon 'will not' and designates that person whose inclination is against earning his living and who prefers to burden others. It certainly does not refer to those who cannot, through incapacity, work nor those for whom no work is available.

let him not eat: the onus is laid upon those who could support such idlers to refrain from doing so (this command, therefore, expounds the disciplinary avoidance of idlers spoken of in verse 6). Paul is maintaining that it is not part of brotherly love to allow a man to exploit the concern and generosity of his fellows but rather that real love will take the form of making it imperative that each person plays his full and responsible part in society. To be sure, the context concerns brotherly love and the duty not to abuse this and does not directly relate to social structure, political theory, or economic systems. Nevertheless, in the two class social structure of the Empire this command must have been as radical as the affirmation of the equality of man in Gal. 3.28, and still presents a radical challenge to capitalism and to the abuses of a welfare state where some, able to work, are allowed by the social and economic system to live from the labours of their fellows. Various efforts have been made to find a previous example of this directive in rabbinic literature or in Greek writings, but without success. It is entirely possible that Paul produced the maxim himself. The view put forward above (on the introduction to verses 6–15) that Paul is dealing with a problem arising from a misunderstanding of what brotherly love involved, rather than a problem concerning 'realized eschatology', is supported by the fact that Paul answers the problem in terms of this maxim; if the idlers were lazy because they believed the Parousia was about to come (as many scholars hold) then we would expect Paul to say something like, 'all must work right up to the Parousia', or 'all must work because the Parousia might not come so soon as you suppose', but there is no hint of such an answer.

11. For we hear: most likely, word had just reached Paul at Corinth about these disorderly idlers. Doubtless there were enough people coming and going between the two cities to enable reports of this kind to travel quickly and easily, and we need not think of a special messenger.

that some of you are living in idleness: we are to think of a small minority group (see the introduction to this section). The construction of the Greek suggests a nuance not reproduced in RSV. The Greek has 'some behave (lit. 'walk') among

you in idleness', 'among you' signifying, as in verse 7, comportment. 'Some live
in idleness amongst you' rather shows up the problem as an open scandal and the
responsibility not only of the idlers but also of those amongst whom they live.
On 'idleness', see on verse 6 and 1 Th. 5.14.

mere busybodies, not doing any work: there is a play on words in the Greek
(which Moffatt reproduces with 'busybodies instead of busy', and NEB tries to
capture with 'minding everybody's business but their own'). 'Mere busybodies'
translates a Greek word, *periergazomenous*, found only here in the New Testament
(though the adjective from the same root is found with this sense in 1 Tim. 5.13
expressively coupled with 'tattlers', and in another sense in Ac. 19.19). The verb
means basically 'to waste one's energy' and so 'to be a busybody'. Some commentators think that the idlers busied themselves with persuading others to abandon
their work in view of the impending Parousia. It is, however, not at all certain
either that these people had abandoned their work because they believed the
Parousia must come within a few weeks or months, or that their meddling in the
affairs of others was more than the natural consequences of idleness. As suggested
in verse 10 above, had the cause of their idleness or the intention of their meddling
been connected with an intense delimited Parousia expectation, we could have
expected Paul to have brought the Parousia theme into this section whereas it is,
in fact, noticeably absent.

12. Now such persons we command and exhort: the idle are commanded,
(cf. on verse 6) but also exhorted (cf. on 1 Th. 2.11). There seems little to support
taking the phrase 'in the Lord Jesus Christ' with the latter verb only (as NEB does)
for both command and exhortation are delivered 'in the name' of Christ.

to do their work in quietness: Moffatt finds three commands, 'to keep quiet, to
do their work and earn their own living', whilst NEB rolls all into one, 'to work
quietly for their living'. The expression 'with quietness' suggests a manner of
behaviour which is to characterize an activity whilst 'earn their own living' (lit.
'eat their own bread', see on verse 8) refers to the result of activity (as in 1 Th. 4.12
'and may have need of nothing'). 'Quietness' translates the noun cognate with the
verb used in 1 Th. 4.11 (which see) and from the context must signify the calm and
contentment which are the opposite of busybodying.

13. Brethren: lit. 'but you, brethren'. Paul reverts to addressing the whole
community.

do not be weary: the verb, *enkakeō*, has the primary meaning 'to behave badly'
in something and thence derives the sense 'to omit to do something' whilst its
regular sense in the New Testament is 'to tire through discouragement' (cf.
Lk. 18.1; 2 C. 4.1, 16; Eph. 3.13). It is used in a similar connection to this verse in
Gal. 6.9, and the particular meaning is that the converts should not allow the idlers
to discourage them from brotherly love.

in well-doing: the verb, *kalopoieō*, of which this is the participle, is found only
here in the New Testament and probably means 'doing what is right' (cf. NEB and
Moffatt) rather than 'doing beneficial deeds' though, in the context, 'what is right'

14 If any one refuses to obey what we say in this letter, note that man, and have nothing to do with him, that he may be ashamed. 15 Do not look on him as an enemy, but warn him as a brother.

16 Now may the Lord of peace himself give you peace at all times in all ways. The Lord be with you all.

17 I, Paul, write this greeting with my own hand. This is the mark in every letter of mine; it is the way I write. 18 The grace of our Lord Jesus Christ be with you all.

---

will have special reference to the duty of brotherly love. Clearly the abuse of brotherly concern by some members of the congregation would discourage the faithful from continuing to display this love but Paul reminds them that brotherly care is *right*; just as it cannot be made more right by being appreciated, so it cannot be made less right by sometimes being abused.

14. Doubtless Paul hoped that those who formerly had walked 'not in accord with the tradition' received would respond to the command and encouragement in this letter; nevertheless he reckons with the possibility that even this further reproof will not be entirely successful and therefore adds a further disciplinary measure which reinforces what he has said in verse 6.

If any one refuses to obey: lit. 'if any one does not obey', the verb meaning basically 'to listen to' (cf. Ac. 12.13 in this sense) but carrying generally the sense 'listen to submissively' and so 'to obey'.

what we say in this letter: lit. 'our word in the letter'. 'Our word' or 'what we say' refers specifically to the commands in this final section. 'This' letter (as RSV, RV, Moffatt, though not NEB) rightly interprets the definite article which signifies this actual letter and not 'any letter in general'.

note that man: the verb used here is found nowhere else in the New Testament and only once (Ps. 4.7) in the LXX. But it is found in classical Greek and in papyri. It means 'to mark well' (in grammar it was the equivalent of our 'nota bene'). There is little to be said in favour of the suggestion that Paul means 'make a note in a letter of whoever disobeys' which ignores the word order of the Greek and the definite article with 'letter'.

and have nothing to do with him: cf. on verse 6. The disobedient are to be avoided. The verb used here occurs elsewhere in the New Testament in 1 C. 5.9, 11, where Paul is also dealing with recalcitrant members of the congregation. It is sometimes said that what is here advocated (to avoid close friendship with offenders) is not so severe as the disciplinary measures of 1 C. 5.9ff. because there it is explained that the faithful should not even eat with offenders. However, it is likely to be precisely this that Paul is advocating in the case of the Thessalonian idlers; the faithful are not to feed them and so encourage them in their laziness! On excommunication see on verse 6.

that he may be ashamed: this verb, *entrepō*, has the basic meaning 'to turn about' which leads to the meaning 'to make one turn about' and thus 'put someone to shame' and also 'to turn towards' and so 'to reverence' (as e.g. in Mt. 21.37). Here, without an object, it means as RSV renders, 'may be ashamed' and provides the corrective purpose towards which discipline within the church is directed; the aim of Christian discipline is not retribution nor vengeance but amendment of life.

15. Do not look upon him as an enemy: this verse helps to make explicit the purpose of church discipline for it explains that brotherly concern must characterize the church's dealings with offenders. The expression is not adversative (cf. RV 'and yet'), the Greek 'and' only introducing a further thought.

but warn him as a brother: 'warn' renders the same Greek verb used in 1 Th. 5.12, 14 (translated there 'admonish') and in the context means something more serious than NEB 'give him friendly advice'. 'As a brother' could mean 'as one would admonish a member of one's family' (so NEB 'as one of the family') but is more likely to mean 'as a brother in Christ'.

CONCLUSION 3.16–18

As in the first letter, Paul closes with a prayer, a greeting, and a benediction.

16. Now may the Lord of peace himself: cf. on 1 Th. 5.23 (and on 'peace', see 1 Th. 1.1). 'Lord' here is Jesus, as throughout this letter. It is the one whose nature is peace and who himself disposes peace who is invoked here to give peace to the converts, in their afflictions (chapter 1), in their problems (chapter 2), and with their awkward members (chapter 3). The prayer is as appropriate to the contents of the letter as that in 1 Th. 5.23 is to the contents of the first epistle. In this sense it is a fitting conclusion. As a prayer it is also a reminder to the converts that it is 'the Lord of peace himself' who can and will achieve his purposes for them.

at all times in all ways: i.e. continually (as Moffatt renders) and under every circumstance (cf. similarly in 1 Th. 5.16–18).

the Lord be with you all: this is really the same prayer as before because the vicarious presence of Christ in the Spirit is that which bestows peace upon the congregation (cf. Jn 14.26f.). It may be that 'all' is emphatic, consciously embracing even the offenders, but it may be quite natural and unemphatic (as in e.g. Rom. 15.33; 1 C. 16.24; 2 C. 13.14; 1 Th. 5.26).

17. I, Paul write this greeting with my own hand: the slightly awkward Greek (lit. 'the salutation with my own hand of Paul') has led to various translations, 'the greeting is in my own hand, signed with my name' (NEB), 'the salutation is in my own hand, Paul's' (Moffatt), 'the salutation of me Paul with my own hand' (RV), but the sense is clear that at this point the writer takes the pen from his amanuensis (see on 1 Th. 1.1 and cf. 5.27) to add a final personal greeting.

this is the mark in every letter of mine: i.e. this is the equivalent of a signature by which the letter is authenticated. Paul has indicated that there was some need to authenticate his letters (see on 2.2) and hence this explicit statement. (The Greek has no 'of mine' here, but RSV is certainly not wrong in adding this; Paul is speaking of his own practice in his own letters. At the same time, examples of secular letters with similar authentication at the close can be found.)

it is the way I write: i.e. this is my handwriting. Moffatt is almost certainly wrong in thinking this refers to the grace which follows (and translates, 'this is how I write: the grace . . .').

18. See on 1 Th. 5.28. In contrast to the first letter 'all' is here added, perhaps with a glance to the idle admonished earlier. Some MSS add, as in the first letter, 'Amen' at this point, being a later addition, as are also the subscriptions 'written from Athens' and 'from Rome'.

Index of Subjects

Index of Greek Words